ANTHONY SUTTON M.D.

SEE IT
THROUGH

H.U.S.T.L.E. for SUCCESS

A portion of the proceeds will be donated to the Covenant House for Homeless Youth

Scripture quotations noted KJV is from the King James Version of the Holy Bible. Used by permission. All rights reserved worldwide.

The Anthony Sutton Communication Group

PO Box 540516

HOUSTON, TX 77254

www.asuttonmd.com.

Photography by Mel Mar Images -Darrell Coleman (Owner) - www.melmarimages.photoreflect.com

Book design by J. Godbee graphic design services - jessgodbeefd@yahoo.com

ISBN 9780615918969

Dedication

I want to dedicate this book to my children Meisha, Rena and Joshua.

- ❖ to my past, current, and future students of MDI Prep Course
- ❖ to the millions of homeless teens across the world

And to all those reading this book, please reach out to a homeless teen today and make a difference.

Thank you

Acknowledgments

As I prepared this book, I focused on the few pieces of advice I could share with students that would transcend any of their economic backgrounds, ethnicities, or other demographic distinctions. While receiving council from a trusted friend, Dr. C. D. Johnson, I became convinced that I should make all of my points practical and applicable. To be sure that is not the only bit of wise advice I have received. I have a seemingly infinite list of people to thank, and I would in no way intentionally leave anyone out. That said, I want to first acknowledge my immediate family. To my mother Debra Cross – thanks for everything. That's the best way I know to sum that up. I also want to thank my stepfather who has played such a monumental role in my development that I refer to him as my "real" father. There were times he put the family through its share of hardships; nevertheless, I learned many things from him. Despite the fact that my grandmother Mabel Cross is gone, I am grateful for her guiding me with her words, instructing me as she stood cooking in the small kitchen that made miracles. Thanks to the entire Sutton and Cross family. To my children Meisha, Rena, and Joshua Sutton thank you for keeping me grounded and focused on seeing it through.

It goes without saying that I must offer thanks to my extended family, Adell Cross Jr. (Pepe), Angela, Ava, and Andre. I am indebted to all of my college contacts at Lamar University, Prairie View A&M University, and McPherson College. I particularly want to pay tribute to my line brothers of Omega Psi Phi Fraternity (Eddison Arnold, Bernard Goudeau, Kenrick Greene and Kevin Semien) for always being a pillar of support for me. I extend a special thanks to Pastor Terry Anderson and the Lilly Grove Missionary Baptist Church for helping me financially so that I could stay in medical school. And I cannot forget to recognize Reverend Carlos Washington, my friend and spiritual mentor, who coached me toward believing in my goals, even in those times when the very act of hoping seemed hopeless. I also must acknowledge a loyal friend, and confidant, who was there for me through the good and bad times – Leanene Garr.

I would be remiss if I failed to thank the following people for their contributions: The McCurley's, Suzanne Senegal and her mother Helen Jones (for their friendship and support), Dr. Howard Lee-Block (for her friendship), Dr. George Brown, Dr. Smith, Dr. Alfonso Keaton, the PVAMU Undergraduate Medical Academy, Beb Garr (making Thanksgiving wonderful with her banana pudding), Darrell Coleman and the six sensational studs of Upsilon Theta Chapter (for wisdom and support), Keith Walker and family (for their friendship), Alpheus Moss (for his financial guidance), Erin Patterson (for her legal and tax support). A host of Science teachers have afforded me the opportunity to see the beauty of the discipline. Among them are Mrs. Ford from Cullen Middle School and Dr. G. Pahlavan and Dr. J. Carey from Jack Yates High School. I am deeply appreciative of my friend and bestselling author and inspiration,

ReShonda Tate Billingsley, who demonstrated for me, at a relatively young age, what is possible for anyone who follows his/her dreams. To my former football coaches and teammates thanks for the unity. To Felicia Baker and the Baker family thanks for everything you did for me and my family. Thanks to the Hawthorne family who kept me in line when my parents were at work. Thanks to my friend Rosalyn Antoine, who started me on my journey by assisting me with drafting and editing my medical-school entrance essay. Dr. G. Marshall, thank you for opening my eyes to a world outside of Houston. Without my book consultant, Shanedria Wagner, this book would not have come to life. She has been an inspiration from the time I read her first book of poetry entitled "Phases." I thank her for dotting all the I's and crossing the T's, not to mention everything else she did to make this happen. Thanks to Dr. Michon Benson for her content editing of the book.

Special thanks to my medical influences, starting with a good friend and the person that introduced me to the world of human anatomy, Dr. Leonard Cleary. Thanks Dr. Margaret McNeese for always being there when I needed you. A special Hookem Horns to the President of the UT Health Science Center, Dr. Giuseppe Colasurdo, for your character and all you do for the students at UT. To my medical school family and mentors, some of which include; Dr. Robin Williams, Dr. Jackie Turner, Dr. Phillip Johnson, Dr. Wallace Gleason, Dr. Maximilian Buja, Dr. Latanya Love, Dr. Safi, Dr. Estrera, Pat Caver, Dr. Philipe Pinel, Dr. Lahoti, Dr. Gunn, Dr. Mark Farnie, Dr. Joe Bedford, Dr. Ike Ogbaa, Dr. Nena Lewis, Dr. Jene Simmons-Holmes, Dr. Kevin Smith and Dr. Judianne Kellaway for their support. Thanks to Orthodontist Dr. Elgin Wells, and Dr. Heather Momin-Brown, for always putting a smile on their patients face. Thanks to Dr. Flannigan for making my trips to see you as painless as possible. And to the many other friendships such as; Dr. Ersoy, Dr. Demetris Green, Dr. Dung Dang, Dr. Kavon Young, Dr. Ruben Mendez, Dr. Brannon George, Dr. Brandon

Fields, Dr. Kenyatta Jones, Dr. Aja Fowler, Dr. Reginald Hence and Dr. Tanya Stephens.

To all my previous and current students of MDI Prep – thank you for being a part of our program. Your achievements were a major inspiration in my penning this book. Last, but surely not least I would like to thank my younger brother, George Isaac Jackson IV (Ike) and my beautiful sister Aquarius. You both were one of the reasons I kept pushing forward.

My journey and trials could have ended in an adverse situation, but it was by the Grace of GOD and the assistance of strangers that I endured. You made all the difference. Some of these angelic strangers came from a wonderful place called the Covenant House of Houston. They took me in as a homeless teen and guided me to unimaginable heights. I am truly thankful to the Covenant House for allowing me to share my story with other homeless teens and all their supporters.

Table of Contents

INTRODUCTION - THE RACE BEGINS

Growing up in a two-parent home does not always guarantee stability. At least that was the case in my house. My parents' financial crises coupled with my step-father's episodes of violence ripped through the fabric of my family.

I never met my biological father: My step-father was the only father I had known during my formative years. He was a well-respected member of the community, and because he was somehow able to keep his alcoholism well hidden from public view, he managed to keep a job and take pretty good care of our family. Despite some of the latent feelings that I have about the way he raised my brother and me, I will always remember the values he taught. He stressed the importance of serving others; how to continue to push for excellence, even when mediocrity was pushing back; and how to be fearless in the face of danger. He might even be surprised to know how much of an impact his lessons have had on me over the years.

My step-father had himself grown up without a father and had dropped out of school in the ninth grade to support his own mother and sisters. Having to grow up fast and never having the opportunity to experience a true childhood, he enlisted in the Marines at seventeen. Oftentimes, my father would recall to my brother Ike and me that his service in the military not only enabled him to serve his country, but was his sole means for supporting his family.

Fast forward his life, passed his military service and divorce from his first wife – he met my mother when she was a young single mother with two children. I was five and Ike was three years old. A secure job at a local grocery-distribution plant afforded him a comfortable lifestyle despite his lack of formal education. The downside was that it also financed his alcohol addiction. For the next 13 years, I came face-to-face with the Dr. Jekyll and Mr. Hyde living in my own home.

While I witnessed countless shouting matches and had my fair share of whippings, I recall two instances, in particular, in which my choices caused my father's wrath to rain down on me. I remember the events as vividly as if they had happened yesterday, and they have both significantly impacted the course of my life.

In the late 1980's, at the age of seventeen, I was homeless and sleeping most nights on hard concrete behind Hartsfield elementary school. Ironically, just ten years prior, I was a student at that same elementary school.

To truly understand this twist of fate, I need to retrace my history back to 1977 or 1978 when heavy rains hit Houston, Texas, forcing schools to close. I recall my mother saying, "Today you all will have to stay home because the school is closed." However, I felt the need to check on this myself and, without her knowledge or permission, I left home in the midst of the hurricane to see if the school had actually closed.

Two things prompted my braving the torrential rains and risking being scolded by my mother. The first was that prior to that storm, I had a perfect attendance record, and I had anticipated receiving the highly-coveted end-of-the-year certificate. I had been waiting all year for that recognition. The second reason, which was more important, was that school had become my safe haven; it enabled me to escape the dangers that lay in my home.

As children, Ike and I suffered child abuse. Punishment in our home was not the occasional time-out or dismissal to our room. In addition to the extension cord whippings, we were subjected to something more mentally devastating. Punishment was often reduced to a choice between receiving a lengthy whipping (that could last several minutes) or what my father called, "getting under that thing." I still shudder at the thought of that. In our kitchen, the counter tops were roughly three feet high and three feet wide. We would store a variety of items on the shelves – laundry products, dust pans, pots, and other kitchen items. We all referred to this location as "under the thing". We were directed to this dark barren place with worn out based boards, spider webs, and rusted nails that pieced the few remaining shelves together. I dreaded kneeling on the broken floor tiles that added intensified an already painful situation.

When I was about seven or eight years old, my father realized that we could actually fit under the thing, so whenever my brother or I misbehaved, or whenever my father felt that we deserved it, we would have to go under the thing and kneel as if we were praying to think about our mistakes. In retrospect, the average amount of time either my brother or I spent "under the thing" was two hours. My longest stint there was ten hours for falsifying a grade on my report card. On my father's grading scale, a "C" was equivalent to an "F," and I was so afraid of being punished, that I changed the grade on my report card.

Imagine how mortified I felt when I got an "F" in English class. Not only was I suspended from the football team, I also had to face the wrath of my father. As soon as I received my report card, I engineered the plan to alter my "F" to an "A". I used a black pen similar to the one my teacher used, and drew a line from the right corner of the "F" downward, creating the

appearance of a boxy-looking "A". I felt pretty proud of my

handy work and had no thought that my parents would figure it

out. I rushed home to show my rigged report card, featuring five

"A's" and one "B".

My mother excitedly assured me that we would have to take

my report card to McDonald's to get the Happy Meal that the

franchise awarded to all honor-roll students. I thought I had

successfully fooled her, yet at some point during the celebration,

my mother took one too many glances at my report card. The

final time, her gaze was a bit more probing; it was the sort of

gaze that made her tilt her head slightly, and it was followed by

an unexpected, drawn-out "hmmmm." "This "A" looks really

different from the other ones, Anthony," she observed.

I was a lousy liar. My mother had an uncanny way of giv-

ing me that better-not-be-lying look that made me confess. My

heart began to race, my palms began to sweat, and butterflies

started a party in my stomach. I would later learn in college that these were indications that my sympathetic nervous system was at work. However, that understanding of biology would not have spared me from the punishment that I would eventually receive.

At the moment of my mother's discovery, I wished with all my heart that she would show me a little mercy and not tell my father about my changing my grade. I was not that fortunate. When my father called home on his lunch break, my mother spilled the beans. My first thought was to flee before he came home, but then I considered that my attempts to run might be short lived.

As I waited for my father to get home from work, I couldn't help noticing the large brown clock on the dining room wall. Its "tick-tock" was louder than I had remembered, and its hands seemed to speed around the circumference of the clock face faster than they ever had. Normally, when a person anticipates something good is about to happen, the clock moves super slowly, but on that occasion that I wanted to prolong my punishment, the clock was my enemy, hurling me toward what I knew would be a painful doom. It was eight o'clock when my

father made it in from work. I knew he would be weary from the

heat of the warehouse where he drove a forklift, but I also knew

that wouldn't stop him from getting to me. I was in the back

room pretending to read and hoping that I wouldn't hear his

heavy footstep tracing the back hallway.

Ten minutes, twenty minutes, and one hour went by, but

there was no mention of my report card. "Maybe he has forgot-

ten about what I have done; he has more things to worry about

like getting the car fixed and taking care of the home," I thought

naively. My hope faded the moment my father barked my name

with his distinctive U.S. Marine voice. "Ant, come in here!"

On his lap lay a white extension cord and a white belt. He

informed me that I had three choices: the belt, the extension

cord, or "getting under that thing." I may have been only

twelve, but I was no fool. I opted to get under the thing. What I

hadn't factored into my decision was that I had grown considerably since the last time I had been sentenced there; I was actually taller than five feet, but the thing was still only three feet tall.

At my father's command, I assumed the kneeling position and got under the thing at 9 o'clock. Around 11:00, I realized that my punishment was not going to be the customary two-hour-long stint. After the four-hour mark, I could no longer feel my knees, and my neck had begun to stiffen.

Bored and isolated, I noticed a small hole at the base board under the counter. Out popped a mouse's tiny head. It must have sensed I was there because it immediately withdrew into its hole. At first I was startled, but I knew I couldn't move because of my punishment. I tore a straw from a broom next to my leg and when the small, furry head popped out again, I quickly touched it with the straw. The mouse retreated, but soon came out again.

We continued this poke and retreat for over an hour until the mouse gave up. Before I knew it, I had fallen asleep and was awakened by kitchen lights and my father's voice saying, "Get ready for school." I tried to quickly rise, but I could not stand straight for several minutes and my neck had become locked to one side. I spent ten hours under the thing that night. That experience taught me that there was no obstacle that I could not overcome. Patience and perseverance were my two greatest allies. I am sure we've all heard the saying everything happens for a reason. This early introduction of facing obstacles began building an interior armor within me that would be tested during high school.

CHAPTER 1

H is for HANDLE YOUR BUSINESS

The second lesson I learned happened a few years later. As a teenager, I resented my father's alcoholic tirades. He routinely drank with his friends, and my brewing frustration came to a head during my senior year of high school. At the time I was a starter on the football team, a member of student council, and at the top ten percent of my class. My scholastic and extra-curricular performance had primed me to go to college on either an academic or athletic scholarship. I remember the day so clearly. It was a Thursday, and my father had been on strike from his warehouse job of fifteen years. Needless to say, this was a very stressful time in our home.

One night, my mother decided to visit a neighbor while Ike and I watched television in the living room. My father asked us where my mother was, and we told him she had gone across the street. Disgusted and discernibly irritated, my father then demanded that we not open the door for her. My mother soon returned and began knocking on the locked front door.

She continued knocking and calling for my brother and me; I sat frozen looking at the door, too intimidated to move. Suddenly, Ike defiantly let her in. At that moment, I questioned my own manhood. Ike, who was two years younger than I, had the courage to do what I could not. In the very next moment, having realized Ike's disobedience, my father returned to the front room, swiftly picked up an iron chimney cleaner, and swung it at Ike's head. Were it not for Ike's quick reflexes and my warning shout to "Watch out!", I'm not sure what would have become of him.

It was in that instant that all the years of anger I had harbored and my sense of duty to protect my mother and siblings converged. I boldly stood up to the man I had feared most of my life, challenging him to step outside. Uncharacteristically quiet, my father made a b-line to his bedroom closet, retrieved a .38 caliber pistol, and returned to the living room. Standing over me, he forcefully offered me a choice: I could either walk out of his house on my own or be carried out on a stretcher.

My mother begged him to calm down and urged me to back down, but my backing-down days were over. "Get out of my house!" he yelled. Ike said he would go with me, and my mother threatened to leave my father. Truth was, there was no place for all of us to go. It was easier for me to fend for myself on the streets than to secure shelter for my mother and siblings. I felt my father's anger was mostly directed at me and thought it would be best if I just left home to neutralize the situation. I walked away with nothing but the clothes on my back.

Drifting for hours on the streets of Houston, I ended up at the elementary school near our home. A wooden building offered some temporary relief from the weather and as soon I sat down on the covered porch, my mind began to replay the horrible scene that had happened earlier. The depth of my f isolation and confusion cannot adequately be expressed. School had always been my safe haven. As fate would have it, the same elementary school I attended as a child offered my only shelter.

The days I spent behind Hartsfield Elementary turned into weeks. I questioned my existence and my circumstances. "Why me?" I thought. I would close my eyes at night, hoping I wouldn't wake up. I didn't want to kill myself, but I didn't want to wake up to the same hard concrete as I had many days before. I had no protection from the elements, no comforts of home. I would remove my school books from my backpack and stuff it with clothes to make a pillow; my t-shirt and pants were my only blanket. Despite my disappointment upon waking in the mornings, I had become increasingly aware of one peculiar truth – no matter the personal challenges I was experiencing, the sun kept rising. Each day, it kept showing up to greet me. It was as if God was telling me "Good morning," reassuring me I was not alone.

I knew I was not going to accomplish anything if I continued to live behind that elementary school, but I didn't know what else to do. Too embarrassed to share my misfortune with coaches or school administrators, I would sit in the local library until closing time. I would read mostly Science books, but later, I became fascinated with poetry. I enjoyed everything from Shakespearian sonnets to the poetry of the Harlem Renaissance. I began to write poetry, modeling the styles of great poets such as Langston Hughes and Countee Cullen.

We have all met people in our lifetimes that have left a lasting impression upon us. Not all of them have remained a part of our lives, but they have shaped who we are. One such person in my life was a librarian whom I have not seen since my homeless experience.

One evening as the library was about to close, the librarian approached me. As he walked towards me, I sensed he was not about to chit-chat about how I enjoyed the facilities. He walked with a discernibly different intention. I considered grabbing my backpack and running before he got any closer, but something told me to be still. I looked into my notebook as if I didn't see him approaching. When his shadow covered my small desk, I tensed up and questioned my next move. Suddenly I heard him say, "Young man, I have seen you here at closing time for the past week. What are you are working on?"

I was relieved by his question: it was easy to answer. I told him, "I'm working on a poetry project for school." I wasn't telling the truth, and I sensed that he didn't believe me. Who could have blamed him? It was fairly uncommon for a young black male in my neighborhood to regularly work in the library until closing time.

"I think you are running from something or someone and I need to call the authorities to help you," he said. Policemen were about as unpopular as neighborhood kids who frequented libraries, and it's ironic that my first real job after graduating college was as a police officer – I will talk about that later – but at the time, I explained to the concerned librarian the whole story. I even confessed to him that I was homeless. Before then, I had not told anyone what had happened; yet, in that moment, I faced the very thing I had been running from for weeks.

Instead of turning me over to the authorities, this man who knew nothing about me or my background said, "Here's $2.00 young man. If you don't have anywhere to stay, take this and catch the bus to the Covenant House for homeless teens. There'll be someone there who can help you." The fact that I was homeless had not dulled my mind. I had always had a head for money and knew that $2.00 could be put to better use than riding the bus. "Why catch the bus?" I thought "I'll save this money and make the ten-mile walk to Lovett Boulevard instead."

I arrived at the intake door of the Covenant House and was greeted by a small African American woman. She gave me a hug, even before asking my name. I'm not sure, but something must have been written on my face that suggested I needed one. I do know that her embrace opened up a flood gate of tears I didn't know I had.

After going through the preliminary intake questionnaire she gave me the rules. She made it clear that the most import rule was that residents could not loaf around the facilities all day. If I was going to receive help, I would have to actively seek and secure employment. I had no qualms about working and immediately began looking for a job.

After weeks of searching, I went to a well-established steak restaurant in Houston's affluent River Oaks neighborhood. I asked the assistant manager if they were hiring; he said that currently there were no openings, but he encouraged me check back in a couple of weeks. Any other time, I might have thanked him and left discouraged, but this time was different.

Before I exited the restaurant, I glanced at the bus boys and noticed they were wearing white buttoned-down shirts and black dress pants. A light bulb went off in my head: I'd take the librarian's two dollars to the local thrift store. With it, I purchased a white shirt for fifty cents and black pants for a dollar.

The next day I entered the restaurant with the two other bus boys and introduced myself to them as the newest employee. They shook my hand and began showing me the ropes. I worked the entire shift at the steakhouse, and for a while, I was able to forget my troubles. I was living in the moment, enjoying conversations with my "co-workers" and serving the elegant guests. Among them was NBA basketball sensation, Ralph Sampson, who was dining with a group of NBA executives.

The waiter for Mr. Sampson's party asked me to be the lead bus boy for their table. I couldn't believe my fortune. I was working a high-profile table at a restaurant where I was not technically employed. As Mr. Sampson prepared to leave, he discreetly called me over and said, "Thanks for the service." He then shook my hand and slapped a one-hundred-dollar bill into my palm.

I hustled from sun up to sun down. Impressed, the manager approached me at the end of the shift and said he was really pleased that his assistant manager had hired me. I admitted to him that I had actually been turned away the day before and had returned to prove myself. Moved by my tenacity and sincerity, he hired me on the spot. I worked as a waiter in that restaurant until I graduated high school.

Take home message: Sometimes be willing to work free to prove yourself, even if there is a possibility you may not be hired.

I could not have predicted that the financial blessings from Mr. Sampson and the librarian would change my life. Being at the right place at the right time and, perhaps most importantly, having the right intentions, made room for a miracle. While living at the Covenant House I began to understand the meaning of charity. I also learned how important it was not to wallow in self- pity.

As an impressionable pre-teen I remember my father spent a lot of time coaching Ike and me through our household chores. I recall the first time he allowed us to mow the yard by ourselves; my father was adamant: "Don't cut someone else's yard before you cut your own."

As a young man, I took the phrase literally; now that I am older, I understand my father's intention; he wanted me to understand that if we were able to take care of ourselves first, we would be of better service to others. Over the years I have watched people, both successful and not-so-successful and I've concluded is that successful people know how to handle their own business. This principle can be learned at a very early age and continually reinforced throughout our lives. When I entered my senior year of high school I was not keenly aware of class rankings, but I did understand that the honor roll meant you were doing well.

The feeling of accomplishment and the accolades I received from teachers fueled my desire to continue to do well in school despite my struggles at home. One such teacher was the incredible Dr. Phalavan, who opened my mind to science.

Throughout the year I maintained a greater than ninety percent average in his class, evidence of my enthusiasm for chemistry. Dr. Phalavan brought the best out of his students. One of the ways he accomplished this was conducting weekly chemistry challenges, typically won by Allen, the class whiz kid. Nevertheless I was always up for the challenge and my goal was to outperform Allen. Of course it should have been loftier, but I was the typical, competitive sixteen-year-old male. Week after week he would outscore me by one or two points.

Finally I decided to put all my focus on preparing for the next chemistry challenge. Immediately after football practice I would rush home to practice chemical formulas, work on deriving equations, and simulate a possible chemistry challenge that Dr. Phalavan might give.

I could not wait for Tuesday morning to arrive and as the bell rang for me to go to chemistry class. The bell was my clarion call to put my game face on. I'm sure Allen was clueless that I was competing against him, but all that mattered was that I knew. The chemistry challenge played out just like I had rehearsed it in my simulation at home. Not only did I beat Allen, I earned a perfect score. Dr. Phalavan smiled, stood before the class, and said, "this is the kind of work that you will do once you are in college". This was humbling and scary. It was scary because I had received a perfect score and accomplished this goal, but never really thought about attending college for anything other than athletics. At sixteen, I asked myself, "Where do I go from here?"

While I pondered this question throughout my senior year of high school, an opportunity presented itself. Chase Bank was conducting a competitive program at Yates High School. The winner would be awarded an academic scholarship to college of his or her choice. I enrolled in it and found myself up against the top ten students in my graduating class. Each week we were expected to complete assignments and perform duties to showcase our leadership skills for points. The student receiving the most points would be awarded the scholarship. Week after week I would perform above average and week after week I would be one or two points behind Allen in the running. Yes, that's right! It was the same Allen from my chemistry class. During the final week of the Chase Scholarship Program there was an assignment due by noon on Friday. This just so happened to be the same week the turmoil at my home erupted and I had begun sleeping behind Hartsfield Elementary School. Despite my homeless situation, I was determined to submit my assignment on time. With no materials or resources to complete it, I waited until the public library opened at 11a.m. and rushed there to begin working. Before I knew it the clock on the library wall read 2:00p.m. I ran to the school only to arrive out of breath and was informed that the Chase bank representative had gone for the day. The deadline for the assignment had passed. Unwilling to accept this fact, I was determined to turn my assignment in. I skipped my final class period (I do not condone skipping) and caught the city bus to the Chase Bank building where her office was located. I was not the most well-dressed student and often times the joke among my friends was that my pants were so short that I needed to pull up my shoes, but that didn't stop me from walking into the beautiful executive suites at the Chase Bank building. With my assignment in hand I presented it to the Chase representative and she was impressed with my tenacity. She regrettably said she could neither extend the deadline nor accept my assignment. As a result, I was three points shy of winning the scholarship.

The days following I began to slack off in my classes. My ninety percent average in chemistry soon plummeted to a seventy-nine. One day Dr. Phalavan pulled me aside after class to discuss my recent drop. I told him, "I'm not going to college, and so what's the point of doing well at this point? I could get a job and make some money. That would be just fine."

Dr. Phalavan, normally even tempered, looked me in the eyes and responded, "Stop making excuses and feeling sorry for yourself. You have the talent to do well in college and if you would just work hard, you may go even further." I thought Dr. Phalavan's words had some validity. So I heeded his suggestion.

A few months later I suffered a groin injury that sidelined me a great portion of my senior football season. As a result, athletic scholarship offers were few. Undaunted, I began to explore other avenues to enter college by completing and submitting applications and academic scholarship packets.

Within a few months I started receiving acceptance letters and academic scholarships to various universities. I finally chose to attend McPherson College, a four-year, liberal arts institution located in McPherson, Kansas. In addition to the academic scholarship, I was awarded a partial athletic scholarship to play football. Spending one year at McPherson was truly a learning experience.

The most inspirational moment was hearing a guest speaker, Alex Haley, the author of the best-selling book and movie, Roots. After speaking to the audience of five hundred, Mr. Haley requested to meet the handful of African American students who were on campus at the time. I, like many of the others around the U.S., saw the movie Roots. If you by some misfortune have not had the opportunity to see this movie, do so. It chronicles Mr. Haley's family history back to Africa. Studded with well-known actors and actresses of the time, it is almost ten hours long.

Now, standing before me was this man larger than life, but only standing approximately five feet-six-inches inches tall with the world marveling at his literary work. At the age of nineteen, I don't think I truly appreciated what McPherson College had done by bringing Mr. Haley to our campus. Five years later, in 1992 he passed away at the age of seventy, but he left those of us who met him at McPherson College some great life lessons. Mr. Haley told us that we should always push for greatness and to never forget to give back.

McPherson was a wonderful university, but I missed Texas and in particular my girlfriend who went to University of Texas at Austin. I decided to abandon my scholarships at McPherson for love to enroll in a university a little closer to her. After visiting Beaumont, Texas and talking with a former classmate from Jack Yates who attended Lamar University, I was sold on attending Lamar. Here is the big twist and not so much a shocker to some. I left Kansas to be closer to my love, but we ended our relationship no more than four months after my enrollment at Lamar. In hindsight I think her maturity and passion to succeed were years ahead of my search to find my purpose in life. It came as no surprise to see her years later as a best-selling author, actress, and news anchor.

During my early college years I was convinced I would become a veterinarian, so as a sophomore, I enrolled in an upper-division biology class without seeking proper counsel from an academic advisor. These classes included microbiology, genetics, and immunology.

I genuinely thought these classes would be interesting. Investigating the microbial world and the life cycles of diseases, as well as exploring myriad ways the human body responds to infection – these learning possibilities drew me in. I loved these courses; unfortunately, they didn't love me back. After investing time and energy into my studies, I earned two F's, one "D", and one "C". I had a whopping .55 grade point average and was placed on academic probation. At that point, becoming a veterinarian seemed like a pipe dream. It was only after I failed that I decided to speak with an academic advisor. I know: I should have done that the first time, but I didn't.

I walked into the office with this professor. Before sitting down, I noticed that he had more plaques on his wall than I had teeth in my mouth. I thought to myself, this is what I would like to see on my wall one day. He had earned a B.S., a M.S., a Ph.D. and a various other honors and certifications. I sat down, expressed my desire to become a veterinarian, and showed him my college transcript.

He said something that moved me in a way that has continually shaped my thinking to this day. He said, "I don't think you are cut out to do something on that level." He calmly and authoritatively explained that I might consider being tested for learning deficiencies. Stunned, speechless, and disgusted, I left his office and sought the one calm reassuring voice I had always gone to – that of my mother. My mother, a sweet and agreeable woman (most of the time) sat and listened to me vent for over an hour.

After I finished my rant, she made an interesting observation. According to her, she too might have questioned my academic abilities had she seen my transcript. She went on to say that if I wanted great things, I needed to be great. I should not wait to be great.

Motivated by her words, I returned to my advisor's office and respectfully gave him an earful. I told him, "While I appreciate your advice, I believe in myself." I went on to tell him that when I started the race to find my purpose in life, there was only one person in the one-lane race. That person was me and that lane was mine. I concluded my exegesis by saying, "With all due respect, I'm the only one who can draw my finish line." I assured him that he had not yet seen my best work and that from that point forward, I would "handle my business".

I identified my first step toward success: surrounding myself with great people in my chosen field and sought out a local veterinarian with a thriving practice. It was a great experience – within the first few weeks of working there, I witnessed heart valve replacements, biopsies, and the wonderful care given to a wide array of animals. However, I soon faced an obstacle while working as his intern.

One day, a gentleman entered the veterinary clinic with his dog named Red. The man had called ahead and had come in to get treatment for Red's severely injured leg. I was busy, helping the client complete the intake forms, and the counter was so high that I wasn't able to get a close look at the extent of Red's injuries. I walked back to the operating room to see the veterinarian prepping the room for surgery, and he asked me to return to the waiting room and bring the animal back.

As soon as I walked through the doors, I got a really good look at Red. He was a huge pit bull with a full set of teeth. They were all visible as he snapped and snarled at my presence. My anxiety was heightened as the owner seemed to have little-to-no control over Red; the dog continuously lunged and snapped his chops at one of the other customers.

I slowly walked toward Red, his eyes focusing on me as though I would make up for several missed meals. I waited a moment for his owner to calm him down, and as I drew closer, he assumed a seated position. Recalling some of the training I had received at the veterinarian clinic, I heard the words of my instructor, "The animals are more afraid of you than you are of them." I turned this phrase over and over in my mind as I inched toward the animal. Each step toward Red felt increasingly intense.

Without a growl, bark, or warning, Red lunged at me when I was within three feet of him. If it were not for my quick feet and my previous experience avoiding blocks on the football field, Red would have surely sunk his teeth into my arm. I retreated to the back room where the veterinarian was completing the set up.

He saw the nervousness in my face and asked what the problem was. I told him that not only did Red not want me to escort him to the back room, this dog was also less afraid of me than I was of him. Without hesitation, the seasoned veterinarian walked to the front and quickly reappeared with Red. Magically, the veterinarian had gotten the Cujo-esque pit to cooperate like a helpless, three-week-old puppy.

At the end of the day, the vet approached me and said that aspiring veterinarians mustn't be afraid of their patients. I realized at that moment that I was not going to be a veterinarian. This brief encounter was one of the monumental turning points in my life.

Abandoning my dreams of becoming a doctor would have been so easy at that point. I could have thrown in the towel, but how could I have achieved success had I done so? How could I have helped others become great had I allowed my journey to

end so prematurely?

Instead of giving up, I continued my race. Shifting my atten-

tion from veterinary medicine, I took a slight detour to a micro-

biology lab at Lamar University in Beaumont, Texas, and began

working as a lab assistant. With no "Reds" in sight, I found a

certain peace, autoclaving spore-riddled petri dishes. I felt

inspired, studying the microbial journals in preparation for the

labs for other undergraduate students. I capitalized on opportu-

nities to travel to various medical conferences with Dr. Hunt, my

new undergraduate advisor. From the start of my apprenticeship,

Dr. Hunt believed I was better than my low G.P.A. reflected.

She would often tell me that if I wanted others to see what I

could do, I would have to give them something worth looking

at. In the fall of 1991, Dr. Hunt invited me to attend a symposi-

um in Galveston, Texas. Assembled there were some of the

brightest minds in medicine, and a large number of them were

my age. I listened attentively to my peers present their groundbreaking research and discuss exciting projects, featuring concepts and vocabulary with which I was so wholly unfamiliar. It caused me to wonder if I had what it took to present on their level.

Despite

I was not always the smartest cookie in the cookie jar;

There were no great expectations on my going too far.

It was the gift of a total stranger that helped me see the light

That I could accomplish great things, despite -

Despite not being born into riches, nor wearing the nicest

clothes;

Learning never to surrender, despite what I was told.

It's easy to give up, when your back is against the wall

The true winner is the one that presses on despite it all

written by Anthony Sutton 2012

❖ **Pearl**: Sometimes things may not always come to you; often times you may have to go get it. (Sutton)

❖ **Pearl**: Sometimes be willing to work free to prove yourself, even if there is a possibility you may not be hired. (Sutton)

❖ **Pearl**: Seek an elder in your community and talk with them about their history and the lessons they have learned. It's worth more than gold. (Sutton)

❖ **Pearl**: Mistakes are not intended to be carried with you daily, but rather to serve as bricks of experience on which to build your foundation of greatness. (Sutton)

❖ **Pearl**: Don't wait to be great. (Debra Cross 1989)

❖ **Pearl**: Those who accept and learn from correction will constantly move toward perfection. (Sutton)

CHAPTER 2

U is for UNLOCK YOUR PURPOSE

A common thread among great people is the ability to unlock and commit to their purpose. There are individuals we have all seen who are amazing high school or collegiate athletes we automatically assume will become professional athletes, but somehow it never happens. There are students at the top of their class who undoubtedly are destined to become CEO's of fortune 500 companies or outstanding doctors, but somehow they never reach this height. What happens along the way to derail their greatness? How do you explain why the number one student in the biochemistry, algebra, or economics class ends up falling short in life?

Some would argue they may have had some tough breaks, or that life may have thrown some unexpected curve balls their way. While that may be true, one thing remains evident. The successful person they could be is chained and shackled by the person they are. I sympathize with the unexpected curve balls such as the loss of a loved one, the birth of child, the loss of a job, the "F" in a class, or an illness. However, according to my stepfather, these excuses are temporary.

He would say "that as long as you can open your eyes, you can see your way out of any excuse". Two of my close friends, Bob and L-Mac, have left this earth, but their words have remained with me. "Excuses are like your mouth. Everybody has one". This not quite how they phrased it, but this would serve as the cleanest version for this book. They were right! We often make excuses for what we either don't want or are unable to do.

Yes, Sarah made straight "A'"s in her science classes and aced her medical school entry exam and should have no problem becoming a physician. There is no doubt that Chris, who scored thirty touchdowns in his senior year of high school should surely have a starting position when he enters college. The reality is that there are some Sarah's who never get past the first year of medical school. There are some like Chris who quit the football team after their freshman year. No one would argue that Sarah and Chris were talented, but some could question whether they were committed.

Talent without the commitment causes one to run an impressive, yet incomplete race. This is not to say they have no drive or true mission; rather, the commitment required to graduate to the next level is locked away in a room I refer to as "comfortable".

Movers, shakers, and those on the rise have found the key to this room and have released their purpose, which has been held hostage inside. There are people who hold their purpose hostage for twenty or thirty years because they feel releasing it may actually take them out of their comfort zone. What they may not realize is their comfort zone is slowly becoming a danger zone. Have you ever stayed in a relationship that was not necessarily the best or most productive for you? You stayed because you were raised to stick it out. You stayed because you didn't want to leave this familiar place for a place of the unknown. You stayed because although it was uncomfortable it was still comfortable enough for you to bear it. Suddenly you find yourself spending years spinning your wheels, but not moving anywhere. Relationships are not the only comfort zones that can morph into danger zones.

We have comfortable jobs that pay the bills, but don't allow us to reach our full potential. Sometimes you find comfort in the lesser you, despite your inner genius saying step outside and take a chance on a dream you have always had. These same excuses may have continued to be my Achilles heel had I not received a life-altering call from Darryl, my fraternity brother from college.

By the time I graduated from Lamar University my G.P.A. was a less-than-stellar 2.67. I was unemployed, my bank account balance was $60, yet as the father of three children, I was responsible for paying $600 a month in child support. Anyone can see those calculations do not add up.

Wrestling with my failure to be responsible and financially secure, I spent a lot of time reflecting on the missteps I had made. This became one of my bricks that helped me to lay the foundation for my future. So as I had always done, I began to pray and meditate. My grandmother Mable Cross always stressed to me the power of prayer. She instilled within me the belief that if you pray without ceasing a change will come. I believed and still do believe in these words. I searched for answers and learned the power of coupling prayer with meditation. Initially my meditation consisted of sitting in the living room of my small one bedroom, shower only, four hundred- square-foot house. With no couch or chair, I sat cross-legged with my palms facing upward as they rested on my thighs. I would close my eyes and instead of hearing silence and peace, I would hear more noise than I would if sitting in grand central station. For weeks I continued this and still achieved no inner silence.

Finally, one day I was so mentally exhausted from job hunt-ing that I returned home and fell asleep immediately. I awoke in a twilight zone, somewhat drowsy yet half-alert. I went to my living room and began meditating and before you knew it I could hear nothing. This lasted for over 45 minutes and was only interrupted by the ringing of my telephone. My fraternity brother, Darrell, had called to tell me the Beaumont Police department was hiring. I considered Darrell's suggestion, but in my heart, I had no desire to become a police officer. It was not my dream job; I knew it was not my true purpose in life. Despite my initial aversion to the idea, once Darrell mentioned that the starting salary was $30,000 a year, my attitude changed. My interest in law enforcement heightened exponentially. I thought, "How difficult could it be to protect and serve my community? That's something that comes naturally. The people in my community would surely not mind my familiar face in a squad car." I can't believe how naïve I was.

The police application process did not go as smoothly as I had expected. Initially, I underwent a background investigation, which included a credit check. At the time my credit cards were maxed out, and I had a car repossession on my report. Finally there was the polygraph test, which I had been warned about by applicants leaving the room. One of the prior applicants sat outside after his test and warned me that if I admitted to doing something unlawful, I would have not been offered a job. However, if I didn't admit to something that was picked up as a lie on the detector, I wouldn't have been employed either. He may have been honestly preparing me for what was to come or he may have been trying to eliminate me as his competition. All I could think of is that everything I did wrong through the years would suddenly come back to bite me and destroy my chances of getting the job. A job I was not to thrilled about in the first place. Either way, I was extremely nervous as I went inside.

As I continued vacillating about the kinds of information I should either offer or withhold, in walked a tall, red-headed football-player-looking man. He had such a serious, dead-pan look on his face, that he shook me a little. He looked like the kind of man who could have wrestled the gator whose skin covered the fancy cowboy boots he wore.

Without smiling, he hooked me up to the polygraph machine and began his interrogation. "Is your name Anthony Sutton?" I answered that it was, and the polygraph line indicated I was being truthful.

"Have you ever driven a vehicle under the influence of drugs or alcohol?" he asked. I felt my heart racing. "If I tell him yes, and I know that's against the law, I may not get the job," I feared. Shakily, I uttered, "No" and nervously watched the polygraph needle jump around like a person walking on hot coals. The officer then asked if I had ever taken anything that did not belong to me. Once again, I responded with an emphatic "no," and once again the needle did its dance.

Finally, after a series of questions, he turned the machine off, looked me squarely in the eyes, and said, "So far, Mr. Sutton, the only thing you have been honest about is your name." I was embarrassed, and my thoughts reverted to my children whom I mentioned in the next breath. I told him I had three children and that job was my way to support them. He then said he had three children the same ages as mine.

Soon, we were laughing about raising children and changing diapers. After about thirty minutes of conversation, he turned the polygraph machine back on and asked the same questions, but in a different way. "Did you drink and drive on your way to the police station today? Have you stolen anything in the last twenty-four hours?" The way he asked the questions allowed me to pass the polygraph with flying colors. That encounter created an almost thirteen–year career in law enforcement for me. I believe becoming a police officer was a piece of my ultimate purpose and that passing that polygraph was a pivotal point in seeing this accomplished.

One point to make here is that the polygraph operator and I could not have come from more different beginnings than an alligator and ant, but finding a common interest or common ground with someone who does not look like you can pay huge dividends in the end. This does not mean you should pretend to like someone, but rather find the good and similar interests and connect on that level.

The years at the police department were filled with exciting moments. I was assigned to special units, sent to specialized trainings and reached moderate levels of success. From the outside in it may have appeared that my wonderful accomplishments at the police department were a result of my natural talent to handle situations.

Bishop TD Jakes, renowned pastor of The Potters House Church in Dallas, Texas, said sometimes people mistake talent for commitment. Just because people are talented does not mean they are committed. The problem is that talent without commitment deprives you and the world of your maximum potential. Over the years I have heard students who were happy to get a "B" in a course because it didn't require much effort and scoff at getting an "A" because it meant having no social life at all. Although they are talented enough for a "B" they are not committed enough for an "A". As I pondered these student sentiments over the years I began to ask myself why are we comfortable with mediocrity? The answer I have come up with is because it's a less painful, less demanding and a less sacrificial road than that of fulfilling our true purpose and stepping outside of our comfort zone.

If you think about who you are on your best days, you would perhaps realize that you are pretty awesome. When it comes to "handling your business" – that is, attending your classes, balancing the household, and juggling a relationship, if you gave it your all, ninety-nine percent of the time you would be successful. Inside of you is a genius so amazing that the only way to explain it is true purpose. This purpose is sometimes tucked away in our comfort zone. Although we may not readily see our purpose, it doesn't change that the purpose is still there.

Albert Einstein says that we are all geniuses in our own right. I appreciate this notion because it suggests no matter what struggles we may have endured that each breath affords us another opportunity to realize our inner greatness and purpose. In many of her public addresses, noted surgeon and OB-GYN, Dr. Jewel Pookrum illustrates a similar point when she references her trips to the Redwood forest in California. She shares that she is constantly impressed by the size and, in particular, the longevity of the monumental structures. She says some of the trees have been around so long that no living person remembers their ever being planted. They have always been and will continue to thrive, she concludes, because the trees have never tried to do anything other than be trees – they don't try to run or form words or eat things they shouldn't – they know their mission, and they fulfill it.

Holding on to painful experiences can block your purpose and is tantamount to your strapping an anchor to your leg and then jumping into quick sand. Undoubtedly, in this scenario, you will not only sink, your descent will also be extremely fast. There are two keys to unlocking your purpose: one, unleash the weight, whatever it is – a painful past, insecurities about failure, or not being good enough, or even relationships with "friends" that may be unhealthy; and two, unload your full potential – focus and deliver it. Climb and continue to climb until you pull yourself out of the quick sands of your past.

I marvel at babies as they speak their first words or take their first steps, or the bird that is just learning to fly. Prior to the talking, walking or flying is only their potential to do so. It is the kinetic energy, the energy of movement, coupled with commitment that allows these actions to take place. That begs the question, if potential + kinetics + commitment can transform a bundle of cells into a verbal or airborne creature, how can we use this same formula throughout our purpose- driven life? The portion of the formula that appears to be most difficult is the kinetic movement and the commitment.

Who would have thought that Raul, a Houston gang member, would be one of the keys to helping me unlock my purpose? As a Beaumont and then a Harris County Officer working the juvenile probation units, the opportunity to change a life was always present. It was in the fall of 1999 that I was working the

gang task force unit in Houston, Texas, a multi-departmental

collaboration to address the growing gang concerns around the

city. I was assigned to the Spring Branch area where gang

members were initiated as young as nine years old. My relation-

ship with them was one of authority, but also one of parental

concern for their well-being.

One night while I was speaking to a group of teens who

were part of a middle school gang (whose name I will withhold

to protect the school), one of the teens, Raul, expressed interest

in leaving the gang. This was not something he could express in

front of the group, so he purposely called me a derogatory five-

letter word that rhymes with snitch to get my attention. Raul was

a short, somewhat husky kid with a slicked back hairstyle that

resembled hipsters from the 1950's. He talked with a distinctive-

ly thick accent linked to his El-Salvadorian background. This was

not my first time seeing him. Normally he was one of the more

respectful and quiet of his gang. "Raul", someone shouted. "You bet not talk to Officer Sutton that way, he is cool people". Not heeding the words of his fellow gang members, Raul continued to shout out obscenities. At this point I was visibly annoyed and immediately escorted him away from the group to find out what was going on. "What is your problem?" I asked. Raul responded by saying he didn't want his homeboys to know he was talking to me about leaving the gang. He explained that his grandmother was sick and he believed the stress of him being in the gang was contributing to her sickness. She asked him to focus more on school and to stop hanging with that bad element. It was tough for Raul to simply quit the gang because the lifestyle was all around him. His cousin Victor and many of his friends who played soccer together were all involved.

There was something about Raul that just didn't fit the mold of gang member, despite his intimidating appearance, even at the age of twelve. Something Raul possessed was an uncanny way to analyze a situation and offer a solution. I found this out firsthand when I offered an education class to the Spring Branch gang members, in an effort to show them they could use their GOD-given intelligence to create some great things.

During the class I gave a scenario where the gang members would have to work together to raise money for a school for disabled children. The challenge was they had no building, no supplies, and no startup capital. Within ten minutes Raul had developed a brief business plan that included several fundraisers, followed by an idea to write letters to business leaders for matching funds.

So it came as no surprise that Raul wanted to leave the gang. The question was how he could do so and save his reputation. I began to help him get involved in extracurricular activities at school, which occupied a lot of his time, thus decreasing the time spent with the gang. While many of his homeboys respected the direction in which he was going, one bad actor named mad man was not so accepting.

Mad man was a little older than Raul, but not as large. He was a wiry kid with a tear drop tattoo on his left eye. Although he had never been linked to any violent crimes, the gang task force unit knew he had the tendency.

One day while preparing a presentation for the Region IV Alternative Teacher Certification program, I received a call from Victor, Raul's cousin. Raul had been shot. I rushed to the scene and actually arrived before EMS. Raul was on the ground with a small bullet hole in his leg and one near his left shoulder, close to the chest. While everyone hysterically tried to figure out what to do, I instructed Victor to apply pressure on the areas to stop the bleeding. I was not sure this would help, but had seen it in the western movies and medical television shows. I figured it was the thing to do. Raul was crying out in agony and begging for us to not let him die. The flashing lights of the EMS truck could be seen in the distance, but Raul was becoming more lethargic by the minute. When the paramedics arrived they immediately secured Raul and transported him to Ben Taub Hospital. I, like many others who were with Raul, didn't think he would survive this injury. Hours later, a young doctor appeared to tell us that Raul must have had a guardian angel watching him because the bullet in his left arm narrowly missed a major artery. The physician went on to say Raul was going to survive.

Tears from his grandmother, as she hugged me and the doctor, unlocked a dream I had for many years while at Lamar University. That was the dream of going to medical school. Thinking about Raul and how the healing hands of the physicians saved his life ignited my interest. Considering the impact physicians have on their community, I made a conscious effort to once again follow my dream of going to medical school.

The years had come and gone and at the age of thirty-one with three school-aged children, I was seriously considering leaving the police department and going to medical school. While some things changed, something had not: my grades from undergraduate school. Even though my grade point average was not medical-school-ready and it had been almost eight years since I had any formal science courses, I still felt this burning desire to try. As always I went to the voice of reason and told my mother, "I'd love to go to medical school, but it seems that I won't get in because of my grades. On top of that I'll be almost forty years old when I complete everything. Without any hesitation she countered, "Anthony you'll be forty whether you go to medical school or not, so you might as well do something you enjoy as you make your way to forty," Unbelievable is the word that came to mind.

I asked myself, "Now how do I turn my previous academic short comings, my academic let-downs into future touchdowns?"

❖ **Pearl:** Potential energy + Kinetic energy + Commitment = Purpose Fulfilled

CHAPTER 3

S is for STEP UP TO THE PLATE

Once you have unlocked your purpose it is important to use all the lessons learned to help guide it. Not only is it important for you to believe in your purpose, it is equally important that you act on it. The Bible says, "Faith without works is dead". Meaning, we can dream and believe all we want, but unless we put actions behind the dreams and use the experiences of our past to guide us, we are simply dreamers.

I was ready to accept the challenge of getting into medical school and as I meditated and prayed about how this map to medical school would be designed, I flashed back to some of my childhood lessons for direction.

"Ant, Ike, and Aquarius, line up for choir practice." At least once a week, my mother would make my siblings and me pretend we were in choir practice, marching us in line from our bedroom.

In the dining room of our home was a large, brown piano that my mother would frequently play for friends and family. Her father had been an amazing musician, and my mother's brother Michael was a Motown producer and artist. When I was a young boy, practicing singing and forming a choir didn't seem too odd for either me or my siblings. My mother would call neighbors over to watch us perform and sing. "Go head Anthony! Sing that song," they would cheer. Their encouragement would make me perform even harder. Ike and I would laugh hysterically when we heard our next door neighbor who we referred to as Aunt Mona say, "Sing it Reverend Ike!"

By the time I was an adolescent at Cullen Junior High, just about everyone in my community who had visited the Sutton/Cross living room had convinced me that I had a good singing voice. One day at school, I noticed an audition banner posted to the cafeteria door. Excited about the possibility of being in the choir I started to practice daily until I felt confident enough to showcase my talents in front of Ms. Chapel, the choir director. Ms. Chapel was in her late fifties. She had a large frame, she was extremely strict, and as a teacher, she was extremely serious about the practice of teaching and learning music.

Just before the auditions commenced, Ms. Chapel told us that each of us would have to sing a solo. "Wow," I thought, "Singing alone was not what I expected." I was only used to singing in a play choir at home, where I had the support of my parents' friends.

The first student got up to sing. Her name was Jackie, and she sang "Amazing Grace." Ms. Chapel was so moved that she was on the brink of tears. Jackie's voice was truly advanced beyond her years. Next up was Kim, who also sang a gospel song that was as inspirational and moving as Jackie's.

After hearing the girls' singing, my confidence was a bit shaken; I didn't think I stood a chance to make the choir if I have to sound like either of them. "Step up to the stage, Anthony Sutton." The classroom accommodated between forty and fifty students. Every seat was filled. As I walked from the nosebleed seats in the very back of the room, down the center aisle to the black piano where Ms. Chapel was seated, my legs began to feel like rubber. "What will you sing for us today?" In that moment, I was so nervous that I totally forgot what I was going to sing. I had to act quickly.

I opened my mouth, and before I realized what I was doing, I had begun to sing the mega hit "Super Freak" by then-famous 1980's entertainer, Rick James. In direct contrast to either Jackie's or Kim's sanctimonious selections, I heard myself singing, "She's a very kinky girl; the kind you can't take home to Ma-maaaa!"

Those were the only lyrics I managed to utter because as quick as a flash, Ms. Chapel grabbed my arm and pulled me in the direction of the football coaches' office. Typically, the coaches were the disciplinarians of the school. She relayed the sordid tale of my "Super Freak" rendition and said I deserved a paddling for being a class clown. Leaving me in the coaches' office, she turned on the heels of her brown leather shoes and returned to the choir room.

"What did you do?" Coach Bean inquired, "What could you have possibly done to make Ms. Chapel so angry?"

"I sang Super Freak for my audition," I said, and braced myself for the worse.

Coach Bean was one of those former football players turned—coach. Students hated to see him when in trouble. A lean, physically fit man in his late twenties, he patrolled the halls with a skinny paddle that resembled a boat oar. When he swung the paddle its frightening sound (as it ripped into a pair of corduroy jeans) could be heard around the entire school. Coach Bean could have really let me have it, but he didn't. Instead he chuckled and said, "I'm about to have football try-outs, so get some equipment and come to the field." After trying out for the football team, the coach told me I had played well enough to earn the position of starting defensive back. Curiously, the day that marked the end of my singing career actually signaled the

beginning of my athletic career. Despite the fact that I had made

up my mind to become a famous singer, I inevitably submitted

to a purpose that I had not foreseen. The bigger picture was that

I stood before fifty Cullen Middle School music critics and sang.

This would have never occurred had my fear of public speaking

not been addressed while at Hartsfield Elementary.

I was in the fourth grade when Hartsfield Elementary an-

nounced that the winner of the school spelling bee would

compete in Washington D.C. if chosen to represent Texas.

Initially, I was not interested; actually, I wasn't quite sure I could

learn the enormous volume of vocabulary. However, my mother

had other ideas. She had a way of not sugar coating anything.

She looked me in the eyes and said "Stop being so scary. At

least give it a try." This chapter could have easily been titled

"Step Up To the Microphone", because that's what I did after

being nudged by my mother. After it was all said and done, I was

the grade-level spelling bee champion at Hartsfield Elementary

School. Imagine a young man going head-to-head with fifth graders and coming out on top. In retrospect, I find it quite ironic to remember the word that won me the spelling bee crown was "handcuff."

As the winner of the local spelling competition, I represented all the elementary schools in my area at the regional bee. My swagger, I believed, would surely intimidate my opponents. This swagger was actually a facade to hide the uncontrolled nerves rumbling inside.

I stepped up to the podium for the first round of words and they asked me to spell incredulous. "Wow, what a tough word," I thought, but I smiled, showed my swag, and began to methodically spell: "Incredulous; I-N-C-R-E-D-U-L-O-U-S. Incredulous." I was so fictitiously confident in my abilities that before the judge indicated I had spelled the word correctly, I started to walk back to my seat.

When I heard my name called for round two, I headed back to the podium. A number of my opponents had already been eliminated in the first round, and my feelings of confidence had morphed into full-blown conceit. "Your word is 'hair,'" said the judge. I almost couldn't believe the panel would follow up my first round word with such an easy word as hair. Had I not been quite so cocky, I might have elected to follow protocol and ask the judge to use the word in a sentence.

I spelled the word "hair" quickly and as I had before, began strutting back to my chair. In mid-stride, I heard the judge's stinging words, "That is incorrect. The correct spelling of "hare" is H-A-R-E, an animal similar to a rabbit, but with longer ears." I felt humiliated, but worse still, I had let myself and my school down.

When I returned to the school the next day, the Spelling Bee sponsors, Ms. Griffith and Ms. Sanders, had arranged a ceremony. During the lunch period, I was welcomed by a cafeteria full of my peers, congratulating me. Ms. Griffith presented me with a certificate and said, "Although you didn't win you shined for Hartsfield today." I was humbled by her words and felt foolish for the overconfident way in which I carried myself at the regional spelling bee. There was no need for me to mask my fear with conceit. Surely others on the stage were nervous as well. But to elevate oneself the way I did, and fall to the immovable ground below is a lot more painful than falling and landing on a humble cushion laid there by those who respect you.

Despite my apprehensions to singing before the students at Cullen or stepping up to the microphone for the regional spelling bee, the ability to meet these fears squarely in the face allowed unexpected rewards to manifest.

This is the same mindset I applied to my thoughts of medical school. I knew that whether I succeeded in getting into medical school or not, I would not go out without at least giving it my all. My first order of business was to increase my undergraduate grade point average. That meant going back to school to take the prerequisites for medical school. I decided to look for an institution with a great reputation of getting students into medical school.

My search led me to Prairie View A&M University, the second oldest public institution of higher education in my home state of Texas. Only fifty miles from my home, it only offered the courses I needed during the day. This posed a problem since I held a full time job.

Oblivious about how the scheduling conflict would be resolved, I knew in the back of my mind that it would be. My supervisor at the time was Nate, a seasoned veteran originally from New Jersey. Although he was much older than I, he was more like a brother than a father or supervisor. Very progressive in his thoughts, he believed we each had a Mount Everest to reach and should consequently exhaust all to get there. I mentioned to Nate my desire to go to medical school and my dilemma with my current work schedule. He told me to give him a day or two to think about it and he would get back to me. Two days later Nate called me into his office and instructed me to close the door for discretion. He began, "Okay Anthony, here is the deal. You come in the mornings from five to seven. Then, you go to school from 8a.m. until 1 p.m. Report back here at two in the afternoon. You finish at eight p.m." I was at a loss for words. I felt his plan just might work. I told Nate I could not thank him enough for helping me out and would never forget his kind gesture.

Early the next morning I made the one-hour drive to Prairie View to meet with an academic advisor. I entered the biology department, immediately struck by hundreds of photos of PV graduates accepted into medical school. "May I help you?" inquired a middle-aged woman wearing a conservative blue blouse and an even larger smile.

"I am Ms. Williams, what can I do for you?"

"I would like to speak with someone about enrolling in classes to help me prepare for medical school," I responded.

She responded, "You will need to talk with Dr. Brown, the head of our department. He would be the one to guide you." She went on to say, "I hope you don't mind waiting because he has a few students ahead of you." I glanced at the other three students in front of me and figured the wait wouldn't be that long, so I would wait. The clocked ticked an hour and thirty minutes, yet there was still one student ahead of me. I thought about leaving, but hadn't driven all that way to leave. Finally, Mrs. Williams told me to proceed. I had no idea how popular Dr. Brown was, but he was more sought after by students than a mega superstar. I walked into his well-lit office, which featured a photo-studded wall of former students.

"Have a seat." he said as he leaned back in his leather office chair. Dr. Brown was one of those think−before− you− speak− kind −of people who slowly deliver their point, which is usually very powerful. He may have been in his early fifties, but had cheated the aging process. He was African American with smooth black hair, probably linked to his Native American ancestry. "So what are you interested in doing," asked Dr. Brown.

"I'd like to go to medical school," I excitedly replied. "Although I am thirty-three, I feel like an eighteen-year-old freshman being introduced to my college advisor." Dr. Brown then began to tell me the history of medicine and the road that great men of medicine have travelled. He detoured in his dialogue and told me about Prairie View before detouring once again to discuss politics. In some uncanny fashion he was able to bring all these points together to finally end up discussing a course plan to get me into medical school. Being blatantly honest, he informed me the road would not be easy.

With three kids and a full-time job, I was ready to buckle down. He completed our hour-long conversation by saying, "If you get into medical school, I will be there to tell you I told you so and If you don't get into medical school on the first try I will be there to tell you I told you so, but regardless of the outcome, I will be there".

At that moment in walked Dr. Howard-Lee, whom Dr. Brown said could give me additional insight into the process. Dr. Howard-Lee was young, vibrant, and encouraging. Within thirty minutes she knew my children's names, my educational background, and vehicle model. Her interpersonal skills were magnetic, causing people to gravitate towards her. "Here is the course work you will need to complete," she said. A quick glance opened my eyes to two years of a full course load. Before I had a chance to doubt myself, a voice of reason crossed my mind. "Stop being scary!" I smiled and told Dr. Howard-Lee I would see her in two weeks when classes started.

My first day of class was not any different than most, aside from the fact that I was the only student in class with my nine-year- old daughter Rena. She was fondly referred to as my mini-me. Most times she stuck to my hip like tight leather pants because with no babysitter I had no other option but to bring her to summer classes with me. Rena and I walked to the front of the classroom and sat in the chairs directly in front of the professor's desk. This was a little different from my previous undergraduate days when I would find the seat farthest to the back and closest to the door.

After the first day of class and my drive home I sat in the living room looking at my homework assignments for Biology 1, Chemistry 1 and Algebra. Each seemed to be written in languages other than English which was my native tongue. Not only was it difficult material, it was substantial. As I sifted through the pages of the five hundred- page chemistry book, I had a fleeting thought of staying in law enforcement.

In walks Rena with a notebook and pencil. "I am going to help you do your homework Daddy." As I began to silently choke on a few tears I planted my feet, opened my notebook, and began studying. Night after night I would study for five to six hours between work and home. My grades were outstanding after the first few months of class and everything seemed to be going well until I was called into to Nate's office.

Nate said that someone had reported to his supervisor the arrangement we made about my attending school and the modified work schedule. It was not violating any departmental rules, but his supervisor was not as understanding as Nate. She immediately ordered him to discontinue the arrangement he made with me.

Nate was obviously disgusted. He spoke with her and informed her of his desire to retire a tad bit earlier than he had originally planned. Nate asked me to meet him at a local restaurant after work. During dinner he told me not to let this stand in my way of medical school. He went on to say that he spoke with Bob in another unit, who agreed to let me work the midnight shift there. "That means you work from eleven at night until seven in the morning and attend class from eight in the morning until three in the afternoon. But it would allow you to attend school without any interruption," he explained.

Wow this would help, I thought, but to maintain than rigorous schedule for two years would be difficult. I accepted the position and within two days I was working the midnight shift. One of the veteran officers, Ray, gave me a rundown of my duties and inquired about the chemistry book on my office desk. After telling him about my desire to enter medical school, I heard Ray utter that medical school is for smart nerds, not people like us. I was offended and concerned that he thought officers were not smart enough to attend medical school. He went on to tell me I was too old for medical school. Normally I would have let his comments slide, but that time I was compelled to speak for the voiceless who had not heard his toxic words. I gave him the scenario of a GPS system that makes a wrong turn every now and then, even after receiving input. I went on to say, "The beauty of the GPS is that it will pull up a message that says re-routing if we tend to get off course. This is the GPS's way of keeping us on track and eventually if we continue to drive we will get to our destination." Looking at me with somewhat of an agitated smirk, he asked what my point was. "My point," I said, "is that I plan to keep driving."

Ironically that morning when I got off from work my car would not start and I had a major chemistry test scheduled. Was this a sign that maybe Ray was right or was this testing my commitment to medical school?

Shine

Let's say it all together,

Let's repeat it time after time

Quitting is for losers,

And I came here to shine.

See I could walk around unnoticed

 And simply stand behind the line,

But that's no place for a winner like me,

So instead I choose to shine.

Oh, I couldn't care less about the obstacles

That stands boldly in my way

I'm what you call an obstacle achiever

Or at least that's what I say

I was built to last, but not the last built,

There were others after me

Some were cuter, some were smarter,

But I am still uniquely me

While some may buckle under pressure,

Don't expect me to unwind

I have one goal when I stand before you

And that simply is to shine.

Written by Anthony Sutton

CHAPTER 4

T is for TURN YOUR MOLD INTO

PENICILLIN

Rummm, rummmm was the sound made by my 1992 Mercury. No matter how much I pumped the acceleration gas pedal, the car would not start. I said one of those LORD why me's that people say when they have no clue about why things are going wrong. About this time I noticed an older Caucasian male named Jim whose car had stalled in the street right near our department building. Jim obviously needed help with all the early morning traffic coming through. I went over to Jim and told him to get inside of his car and steer while I pushed it into our parking lot. Once inside the parking lot he thanked me and said he didn't know why his car stopped and it had never stopped on him before. Laughing I pointed to my car, which was one space over and told him my car would not start either. How funny! The car impaired helping the car impaired. I didn't know much about cars, but asked Jim to open his hood so I could take a look. When he did, I noticed his problem was simple. His battery cable had detached from the battery and with a simple connection it started right up. Jim offered to give my battery a boost and see if it would start my car, so I attached the cables from his car to my car and within a few seconds, voilà, my car started.

When I decided to help Jim I had no idea he would end up helping me as well. This random event was confirmation that I was not to give up on medical school or throw in the towel just because I had a minor setback. This taught me something more valuable; we are put on this earth to be a blessing to others.

My grandmother, Mabel, was a very spiritual woman, and whenever an occasion called for wisdom, she would not hesitate to open the Bible. One of her favorite quotes in the "good book," as she called it, was "Give, and it shall be given back to you," and she would always punctuate that sentiment with, "But,

Baby, don't give if you don't really want to." When I was younger, I never really understood grandmother's insistence on adding
to the scripture, but now, I realize how important her words
were.

It may seem counterintuitive, but the best way to achieve
what you want in life is to assist other people to get what they
want and to do it without an agenda. I am convinced that even
from our misfortunes we have the ability to create fortunate
outcomes for others. The first task is to turn our mold into
penicillin.

Most would look at mold on bread or fruit as some unsightly
annoyance. Obviously no one brags about the bread mold at the
dinner table. It was this same mold that Alexander Fleming used
to produce penicillin. Fleming saw the benefit of taking something with little or no value and transforming it into something
that would heal bacterial infections and nearly eradicate syphilis.
How many times in our own lives have we been faced with
moldy situations? We sometimes ignore the benefits of some-

thing unattractive or seemingly useless. Mold is heaven's way of showing us how we can take something seemingly useless and make it useful. Through the years we have heard great stories about individuals who have learned to turn their mold into penicillin. They have learned how to turn the harm into healing.

There is the story of Oprah Winfrey, whose early childhood, with molestation and abuse, became an early mold. However, she was able to call upon her inner scientist and turn that mold into a billion–dollar industry. The HARPO production and OWN studios are the penicillin to millions who dream of greatness. We need not look simply at celebrities for instances of turning a menace into a miracle. We have stories in our own neighborhoods. I would not be surprised if you, the reader, can recall an instance when you have turned your own molds into penicillin.

My earliest examples of this date to the Christmas of 1978. On that day, multi-colored lights covered the tree and the smell of collard greens and sweet potato pie filled the house; yet, something still marred the picturesque scene: there were no presents under the tree. In the days leading to Christmas, my father had a sit-down with my brother and me, and he told us plainly that the family was going through hard times and that he would not be able to buy us any presents that year.

I had never seen my father exhibit tearful emotion, but that day, both my brother and I could see pain in his eyes. For the first time, I was able to connect with him in a way that transcended the fear I usually felt in his presence. My mother encouraged us to make the most out of this Christmas; she reminded us that it was a season to give. She had to go to the store to purchase additional dinner items she had forgotten, and while she was there, purchased two rolls of colorful wrapping paper. When she returned home, she gave us the wrapping paper and suggested that we bless someone else with what we already had. My mother was teaching us that despite this being a moldy Christmas that was no reason for us not to give a therapeutic shot of penicillin to someone else.

At the time, I owned a children's book entitled "Curious George" that my brother loved to read. I used some of the paper to gift wrap the old book, decorated a small, hand-made card, and taped it on the front. It read, "To Ike, from Santa." Ike wrapped the plastic watch he loved so much. The one he wouldn't go to sleep without. On the outside of the package he wrote, "To Ant, from Ike." Early Christmas morning before our eyes were completely open, Ike and I jumped from the bed and ran to the living room. Although we knew there would be no additional presents, but that did not lessen our excitement. Under the tree were two presents, one for Ike and one for me. Of course we knew who had given us our present, but it did not diminish the thrill we got from ripping open the packages on Christmas day. Later, as we sat at the dining room table eating Christmas dinner, I asked Ike why he wrote "To Ant from Ike" instead of writing "To Ant from Santa." He said, "Just in case you didn't like it, I wanted to let you know where to return it."

I have been fortunate to have had two important careers wherein helping others through moldy situations is the mainstay, first as a police officer, then as a medical professional. While at UT Houston medical school, my one goal was to become a great physician. I was in awe as I saw the medical intelligence and wonderful interpersonal skills the seasoned physicians, such as Dr. Mark Farnie, Dr. Phillip Johnson, Dr. Pinell, and Dr. Eugene Toy exhibited. One day, during my first year of medical school, an alumni lecturer, Dr. Kevin Smith, addressed the class. He was a board-certified Ear, Nose and Throat specialist as well as an expert in plastic reconstruction. His lecture was amazing, but his willingness to reach out and help students was even more impressive.

Like so many other UT physicians, Dr. Smith was more than happy to allow students surgical and clinical exposure. It was common practice for him to invite students to scrub in on a surgical procedure or shadow him at the clinic. A brief visit to his office and a glance at his former patients' before and after photo's really tells the wonderful story of how the hands of Dr. Smith can turn their physical molds into self-esteem-building penicillin moments. In my time with him, I gained a real sense of what it would take to become a leader in the medical field.

When I finally reached my fourth year of medical school, I experienced a life-changing moment. I was working in the medical unit at the Harris County Jail. Each day I would walk in, display my student badge, and begin treating twenty patients – my usual load. One particular morning, I was talking with an inmate about his insomnia and seizures.

As I was walking over to my attending physician, Dr. Ho to discuss this patient's condition, I suddenly felt a warm sensation throughout my body. It worked its way from my head through my abdomen and finally down to my feet. The room seemed to spin. My heart raced, and my hands began to shake. I had no idea what was happening, so I called on one of my medical school colleagues who was nearby. Sarah, a good friend and brilliant medical student, came quickly to see what was wrong.

She ushered me into an examination room and began taking my vitals and asked another student to call for Dr. Ho.

Both the EKG and my preliminary lab tests were inconclusive. An experienced nurse walked into my room and calmly asked a series of questions which, at the time, seemed wholly unrelated to my condition. "How are things at home, Anthony?" she inquired. "Have you had any stress in your life recently?" Finally she said," You could be having a panic attack."

This seemed impossible: I had endured more stressful situations than preparing for my board exam or completing a few medical rotations. Regardless, all symptoms indicated Nurse Graham was correct. She suggested that I close my eyes and think of a place that I could walk barefoot without interruption. I initially thought this was odd, but I was willing to try anything at this point. After about an hour, I began to feel like myself again. Later that evening, as I was getting into my car, I experienced the same overwhelming feeling.

For me to label the sensation "fear," would not adequately describe how I felt. It was breathlessness, a loss of control that is virtually inexplicable. I immediately sought advice from Steve who was a first-year resident in psychiatry. He instructed me to practice some relaxation techniques. On a daily basis for the next couple of weeks, I practiced these techniques, but I continued to have the panic episodes, and worse still, they were interfering with my medical-school rotations. Nevertheless, I stuck with the process, and slowly, I learned how to sense the anxiety coming and reverse them on my own. I purposed in my mind that I would not run from this problem and as far as medical school was concerned, I would *See It Through*!

My bout with anxiety lasted for several months until the episodes became less frequent and then disappeared altogether. In the time that I was wrestling with my body's involuntary responses to stress, I also witnessed a dramatic change in my attitude. I stopped stressing over board exams, and I started to accept life for what it was. To be sure, I was not happy with all my decisions, but I stopped beating myself up about them. The beauty of that experience opened my eyes to the fact that my purpose in life is not to solely think about me but to yield to a greater purpose.

Once I had freed myself from panic, I knew that I wanted to help others reach their dreams. Although I could help hundreds or even thousands by practicing medicine, I could help millions by facilitating opportunities for future leaders in the health-care industry and practioners. With the idea and no real way to visualize how it would come to fruition, I began to pray and meditate.

Soon after having my epiphany about helping others, I was approached by a student who was seeking my help applying to medical school. He had applied and was rejected six times. After working with him to improve his MCAT score and coaching him on ways he might market himself to admissions committees, I beamed with pride when he finally received the acceptance letter he had been waiting for. The satisfaction I got from his success was as all-consuming as the panic attacks I had experienced when I had been focusing too much on my own affairs.

Without realizing or even expecting it, my helping that one student in 2008, facilitated the growth of MDI Prep, my medical educational consulting business that has assisted over five hundred applicants with acceptance to medical or dental schools throughout the United States. Ever-expanding, its scope is international. Now my teammates and I coach more than 100 students per year.

Also noteworthy is a speaking engagement at the University of North Texas, during which a professor overheard me talking to a few students and requested that I share my story with an even larger group. Little did I know this was preparing me for one of my most memorable speaking engagements.

In the summer of 2010, an unforgettable speaking engagement led to a culminating speaking opportunity. This was almost twenty years after sleeping behind Hartsfield Elementary. Kevin Ryan, President of Covenant House, personally invited me to be one of the guest speakers at the organization's annual gala. That year, the event was held in New York City and honored former first lady Laura Bush. Over 1,000 people attended, and Covenant House raised money for homeless teens all over the country.

I remember standing outside the five-star Mandarin Oriental hotel, reflecting on how God, through the generosity of strangers, had brought me such as long way. At the hotel my daughter and girlfriend posed for pictures with other guest, such as pop-music superstars Chris Brown and Bow Wow. I decided to sneak out and visit a local homeless shelter.

I approached the front desk and requested to tour the facility. The caseworkers on duty informed me of their strict visitor policy and requirement that I contact the administration office on Monday morning. I understood the shelter's policy better than most people, and as I began to leave, one of the caseworkers came from behind her desk and inquired, "Are you Dr. Sutton?" I told her I was. Then she said she had heard a lot about me and that the residents would love to meet me. She asked me to make myself at home in the common room while she rounded up the teenagers. Approximately twenty minutes later, I was surrounded by beautiful young people who had become homeless for various reasons. We sat together, having breakfast and sharing stories.

"When you were homeless, what did you eat?" a tall, thin-framed young man asked.

As I considered his question, I realized how many memories about that time in my life that I had suppressed. I began to recall the times my younger brother had brought me cans of Spam and soda for dinner. I remembered thinking that, in those days, Spam was the best meal on earth.

In that pivotal time, aspirational thoughts occupied my mind. Despite having neither money nor shelter, I was wealthy with desire. Every now and then what seems to have no value to us is the very thing that offers the greatest assistance. While Alexander Fleming is the most notable individual who identified the benefits of penicillin from mold, he was not the first to under-stand the benefits of helping others. The unassuming mold on bread and other products in all reality should serve no purpose, but what comes from this is a wonderful antibiotic that cures the sick. The same is true for the mold that has been present at some point in your life. It has healing properties. If not for you, then definitely for someone else.

Selflessly helping others is essential to advancing your own success. My classmates took time to help me through the medical panic attack. The student affairs at UT Houston Medical School had the patience to see me through this trying time and give me the support to graduate from medical school. There are countless others who helped me to grow MDI Prep to a level that continuously serves to propel students to their dreams. I keep these people and experiences close to my heart and travel with them as I speak across the country.

Jim, whose car stopped in front of my building appeared to be a moldy event, but he turned out to be my penicillin. The healing that my vehicle needed to make it to Prairie View in order for me to take my exam. The Christmas of 1978 and the lack of presents could have been mold-like, but instead it created a penicillin memory for Ike and me. We laugh about and pinpoint this time as one where we learned to become givers instead of strictly receivers.

In all these instances it should be noted that we focused more on the penicillin than mold.

❖ **Pearl:** Giving is something we all have the ability to do. The newborn gives his parent a smile or unsolicited grunt. The trees give us oxygen without asking for anything in return.

CHAPTER 5

L is for LEAP WITHOUT REGRETS

When I was in college and before every test I would get super nervous, so nervous that I would release natural gases into the atmosphere. Now most times this went unnoticed, but there were a few occasions that alarmed my classmates. Don't judge me. Dr. Sutton is a real person just like you. I realized this was anxiety. How many of you have ever been a little anxious before a big exam?

It is important to overcome fake fear, what most of us call anxiety. This fake fear is based on a perceived outcome that may never come true. I am sure that if an untamed hungry bear ran into your room you would have some fear, but that's real fear. Because it's a good possibility the bear would eat you. A good example of fake fear is when you see this beautiful person that you would love to approach, but you are afraid to approach them because you fear being rejected with a quick, "no or go away. True enough, they may say go away, but that same person may have been waiting for you to approach them many weeks prior. Fake fear causes you to create a negative conclusion before the story has even begun. Regardless if we fail or not, the greater victory is that we never gave up.

The successful person, according to Winston Churchill, can go from failure to failure without losing enthusiasm. I have told my children when they take classes or tests to compete at all times, not against the other students in the class, but against their highest standard of excellence. I want your best. My daughter Meisha asked what would happen if she failed her test anyway. "If you beat your best you in effort and preparation, look at the "F" as a victory," I replied.

While Faith, Failure and Fear all begin with the letter "F", that's where their similarities end. I have been honored to be around many wonderful students since founding the MDI Prep program in 2007. While stories of overcoming struggle and reaching goals can be seen among many of them, one story stands out in particular.

One Friday evening I was at my office around 3pm when Tuan, a young Vietnamese man came in to inquire about our dental exam preparation course. Normally our office is closed on Friday, but I just happened to be there working on a lesson plan. Tuan was about 5'7, slender build with wrinkled clothing and shoes with worn out treads. Initially I thought he was coming to replace our empty water cooler containers. How presumptions of me! "The empty cooler is in the back", I told Tuan, as I pointed to the opening that led to our back offices. Smiling and not appearing offended at all he says, "My name is Tuan and I graduated from the University of Texas in August. I wanted some information about your DAT (dental admissions test) course". With embarrassment mixed with an apologetic drawn out "Ohhhhhh" I asked him to have a seat. While he could have sat comfortably back in the leather office chair, he chose to sit more on the edge with a slight lean forward as if he would have to leave in a hurry. As a customary practice I asked Tuan to tell me a little about himself. Tuan indicated he was the oldest of 7 children and they all lived in a two bedroom apartment with their parents. His father worked 80 hours a week with a salary that was illegally below minimum wage. Tuan indicated he always wanted to attend dental school, but was afraid of failing on the test or failing in dental school. According to Tuan, if either happened he would not be able to support his family like he would prefer. I began to tell him a story about Faith and Fear that went something like this:

Faith and Fear were in a race and Faith was clearly ahead as they made the turn. This race was for the gold and there would be no award given for second place. Suddenly, Fear began to catch Faith and once alongside Faith, Fear tripped Faith, causing Faith to fall with more than 50 meters to go. Fear crossed the finish line with a record setting time. Faith sat on the ground for a minute and finally decided to get up and finish the race. Those in the audi-

ence questioned the point of finishing the race when Faith would not receive an award. Nevertheless, Faith pressed on in pain and agony and crossed the finish line. As Fear was preparing to receive his gold medal an official came to the awards table and informed the committee that Fear was to be disqualified for running into Faith's lane. Faith was then awarded the gold medal instead.

Tuan looked a little confused at the end of my story. I am not sure he got the point I was trying to make, so I told him that it is not uncommon to find faith and fear present at the same time. It is also not uncommon to be overwhelmed by fear when an obvious outcome is not so obvious. I went on to tell Tuan that despite it all persistent faith will always come out victorious over temporary fear. He smiled and said, "That's deep".

Tuan had just begun a new position as a dishwasher at a local restaurant. "Where do you see yourself in 4 years, I asked". As he pondered my question, he suddenly redirects his eyes away from me and to the photo on the wall behind me. Tuan said, "I see myself going there". There was the UT Houston Dental

School. That is a great choice I told Tuan, but you will need to work hard to get a good DAT score. I continued on by explaining the MDI Prep program and how we could help Tuan with his DAT preparation. I told him about the start date and the cost of $1,000 which is required before the first class day. "I don't have $1,000, but I really need this class to help me get into dental school", Tuan said. I told Tuan that while my heart goes out to his passion for dentistry and his enthusiasm for joining the course, it would be unfair to all the other students that paid if I made a concession for him. I informed Tuan that currently we have 9 out of 10 of our seats filled for the current class and once we are at capacity, we direct other students to either another prep course or have them join the following semester. He pleaded with me to save him a spot and give him until Monday to come up with the money. I agreed and as he left he shook my hand like a person that was just given a lottery check worth a million dollars.

Monday evening arrived and at 5p I left the office for the day, but no word from Tuan. Early Tuesday morning I received 3 calls from students interested in signing up for the dental prep course. I had forgotten to get Tuan's phone number on Friday, but something in me really wanted to reach out to him before we filled our final seat. Discussing Tuan's situation with my staff it was agreed that since we did not receive a confirmation from Tuan on Monday we could no longer hold a seat for him. We accepted Carol, a vibrant junior Biology major from the University of Houston to fill our final seat.

Tuesday's workday was coming to a close when there is a knock at the office door. "Come in Mrs. Cross, my mother and office manager, replied. I could hear the communication exchange from my office, which was the next wall over. I am Tuan and wanted to meet with Dr. Sutton. "It's a pleasure to meet you Tuan, I have heard some great things about you", said Mrs. Cross. She had a motherly love and disposition she carried to the MDI Prep office. This would always tend to help anxious students feel at ease. Mrs. Cross calls out, "Dr. Sutton, Tuan is here to see you". Tuan came into my office and began to apologize for not calling me on Monday. He said he was working an extra shift to get the money necessary to start the class. Regrettably I told Tuan we already filled the seat and that we physically don't have any empty chairs in the class room. What if I bring my own chair said Tuan. Even if you did that, we still have the issue of the $1,000 for the course. At that moment Tuan reached into his torn backpack and retrieved a white envelope. Inside was an assortment of $1, $5 and $10 bills that added up to $900. Where did you get the money for the course I asked, considering the different denomination of bills inside? Tuan smiled and said this was from my tips at work and money my dad was saving to buy a car for the family. He said I want to pay all of my course tuition and then pulls out two large Ziploc bags filled with quarters, dimes, nickels and pennies. He assured me that it totaled to $100.

There was no way I could accept this money, knowing the struggle behind it. I decided to create my own Tuan scholarship fund. I told Tuan that I wanted him to find the most clean, crisp $1 bill in the envelope because his scholarship just kicked in and he would need to pay the application fee of $1. Tears began to roll down his face and he sat for almost a minute without saying a word. While he appreciated the gesture, he was determined to give me the money. I accepted the money and informed Tuan he would be our 11th seat. The only stipulation is that he would have to bring his own chair. He laughed, agreed and left my office after giving me a victory high five hand clap. Uneasy with my decision to accept the money from Tuan I went to the bank and got a cashier's check for $1,000. That same day I drove to the address he listed on his new student contact form.

As I drove through the pot hole ridden drive way of the apartment complex I gazed from building to dilapidated building looking for apartment 422. When my mother moved to Houston from California we lived in conditions similar to this one, so I was not surprised as suspicious eyes were upon me as I walked through the apartment complex in my blue business suit. Finally I found apartment 422, knocked on the door and Tuan's mother opened the door, not knowing who I was. I began telling her I wanted to bless them with a gift and it was obvious she didn't understand what I was saying. She called for her 10 year old son to come to the door to translate what I was saying in English to Vietnamese. After he explained this to his mother, she asked her son to ask me why. I responded that it's just my way of giving back. I never mentioned the real reason was because I was so impressed with Tuan's drive and motivation and willingness to make a financial sacrifice to reach his dreams.

Tuan completed his course with us and was accepted into dental school as planned, but went to Dental School in California instead of Texas. In 2012 an invitation to Tuan's graduation came to my office. Enclosed was a round trip ticket to Los Angeles California, complements of Tuan. Attending Tuan's graduation was like attending one of my very own children's graduations. When I walked into the auditorium I was greeted by Tuan and his parents. His mother began saying something to Tuan and Tuan said, "Dr. Sutton my mother said you look like a man that came to our home years ago and gave her a check for a $1,000". I made the joke that I guess I have that kind of face. The years had passed and with her English much better now than 4 years prior, Tuan's mother shook my hand and said thank you for the $1,000 and thank you for helping Tuan. After Tuan had faced his fears and latched securely on to his faith he leaped right into dental school. The years prior to meeting me, Tuan led a life that was setting the stage for him to go to dental school. Before you can leap into your destiny there needs to be some mental preparation first.

One of the most interesting aspects of the Olympics is the spring board and high dive contest. The athleticism exhibited by these individuals is mind boggling. What we see on television is the finished product of years of training. As the diver approaches the edge of the 33 foot high platform the only thing seen is a small body of water that looks like the size of a bathtub. What must be going through their minds at this time? Regardless of the thoughts one thing is for sure, when they begin the bounce on their toes and thrust themselves upward the sheer leaping takes courage. I have yet to see a diver leap and then think mid-air that they want to go back to the platform and propel themself back to the starting point. Our lives are not very different than the Olympic divers. We make that commitment to leap then we should (1) prepare in advance and (2) don't think about going backwards. Preparation is the key and it should start as early as possible.

Dr. Judianne Kellaway-Mason is by far one of the most inspirational speakers I've heard. She is an ophthalmologist and former dean of admissions at UT Houston Medical School. During my years as an interviewer for UT, I would often be a co-speaker with Dr.Kellaway at different colleges. She had this wonderful presentation of a shoebox that guided students on how to prepare early for their dreams. The shoebox was a place for students to keep all their accomplishments, activities, and life experiences. Dr. Kellaway would say students with busy lives will sometimes forget about all the wonderful things they have done and even forget about some of the obstacles they have overcome.

This shoebox is what would help them answer very important questions on the medical school application. Students would sometimes express a fear of the competition in medical school and she would tell them that sometimes you have to focus on being the best you, have faith, and just leap in. I think this shoebox is not only applicable to pre-health students, I think it can serve a purpose for anyone. Inevitably we will one day doubt how wonderful we are, but it is during these times that we should pull out our shoeboxes and look at what we accomplished. It is during this time that we should witness what we have overcome.

When we first started the MDI Prep program we enrolled a pre-dental student who some would consider non-traditional.

She was almost 40 years old, and had achieved a high level of success in her career as a software developer. One day she called me and said she heard about our program of helping students get in to dental school and wanted to know if she could meet with me. We met for lunch and she began telling me that despite her financial achievements she still remained unfulfilled.

To add to this was the fact that she was going through a trying divorce where she felt she was a failure. She came from a family that did not believe in divorce. Her parents had been married 40 years and her grandparents were married for 65 years. Tears begin to rush down her face as she continued to tell me about wanting to go to dental school, but no one believed that was a good financial decision. With a house note, children, and other bills looming, she was advised by others to continue business as usual. I asked her one simple question, "Who draws your finish line"?

She said, "I draw my finish line". With that, I told her to run the race as she saw fit.

"But what if I fail and fall on my face?" she asked.

"Then fall, but fall with your arms spread wide. Just in case you learn how to fly on your way down", I said. "But don't give up."

It is said that faith is the substance of things hoped for and the evidence of things not seen. My words to her were that when you have prayed about it, meditated on it, and feel peace regarding your decision, leap into it without regrets. This wonderful woman took my advice and not only got accepted into dental school, but also worked things out with her husband and remains married today.

The word leap means to jump or spring to a great height. The leap of faith you accept will do just that, spring you to great heights. I know fear can try to creep its way in, but remember what I said about fake fear in the previous chapter. Haters may try to discourage you, but remember what I said in chapter three about unlocking your purpose. Sometimes you may have to stop thinking about it and just do it.

Shoebox

Take a deep breath and hold it

Now everything that has held you back,

Unload it

Because you were born to be a winner

You did not come here to lose

Are you ready to run the race?

Are you ready to set the pace?

Will there be obstacles along the way?

Will others quit while you stay?

Don't quit

You did not come here to lose

To those that doubt you, let them doubt

To those who pout about your success, let them pout

Because you are a winner and didn't come here to lose

Remember that breath I told you to take?

Release it

To the genius you have inside of you

Unleash it

Because you are a winner and

You did not come here to lose.

Show the entire world your greatness

You're the pinnacle of power and prestige

You are the tip of the very iceberg

You are what they have come to see

As you pass near a mirror

Briefly glance at what you see

You will soon realize the world is your mirror

Reflecting your destiny

YOU WIN!

.

Dedicated to Dr. Kellaway

The students still use their shoeboxes.

CHAPTER 6

E is for ENCOURAGE YOURSELF DAILY

Low self-esteem can be a major setback to any admissions interview and moreover, it can be a dream buster. Over the years I have worked in industries where communication is a must. Speaking with victims as a police officer and calming patients while on hospital rounds all required appropriate communication skills. What typically accentuates these communication skills is a positive attitude about both the individuals and yourself.

Growing up I went to a middle school where we would partake in this daily lunch ritual of ranking. Ranking has been called by other names such as shooting the dozens and capping, but it is a way for two people to say derogatory things about one another to illicit the most laughs. I never participated in ranking because I knew I was a pretty easy target. My clothing was five years behind the other students, I ate free lunch, and to make matters worse I came to school with a Jheri curl that I tried to do on my own.

For those of you who may not know what a Jheri curl is, according to Wikipedia it is a permed hairstyle that was common and popular in the African American Black Canadian and Black British communities, especially during the 1970s and 1980s. The Jheri curl gave the wearer a glossy, loosely curled look. A Jheri curl required a two-part application that consisted of a softener (often called a "rearranging cream") to loosen the hair and a solution to set the curls.

In those days it cost around $50 dollars to have it professionally done. I went to my mother and begged her to give me money for a Jheri Curl. She said, "Why spend money on a Jheri Curl when I can do it free." At this point I didn't mind; all I wanted was to have my fresh Jheri Curl for school the next day. The night before my mother went to the store bought the relaxer $3, used her normal setting roller $0, and bought a scarf and bag for me to cover my curls as I slept $1.50. What came from this experience was priceless. The next morning I arose with anticipation to see my new Jheri Curl. Rushing to the bathroom I began taking the rollers out of my hair one at a time, but noticed the curls didn't look like the ones in the magazine.

After all the rollers were out I stood in front of the mirror and I looked like a bad female impersonator with large dry curls. My mother, in her nurturing way, assured me that my hair looked fine. She went on to say the curls were large then, but as the day went on they would start to fall and look normal.

She sprayed some Jheri Curl activator on my hair and sent me to school. Every step taken toward Cullen Middle School, I was hoping, meant one more step to my curl looking normal. Finally I arrived, ran towards the restroom to see what my curl looked like and before I could enter it, one of my classmates looked directly at me with a laugh that he could not contain and said, "Excuse me ma'am. Have you seen my friend, Anthony"? And so the laughs and the jokes lasted the entire day.

This somewhat damaged my self-esteem and discouraged me from being involved in the ranking games at lunch. Well, during one lunch period a beautiful classmate name Cynthia, came to my table and said she wanted to rank. How could I say anything about one of the most popular and well-dressed girls whose parents drove a new BMW?

At the time I didn't know she actually liked me or that this was her way of trying to talk to me, so I said I didn't want to rank. She then said something that made the entire cafeteria burst into laughter.

I had a pretty large gap in my teeth, which was a genetic blessing from my biological father whom I never met. The gap was so large that I could actually fit another tooth into that space. To add insult to injury, there was a famous retail store whose theme song contained a line that read, "fall into the gap". My future girlfriend, but then current tormentor, began saying, "fall into the gap." This phrase rippled through the entire cafeteria.

I came back with the only rank I could think of which was, "that's why you're going to fall in love with this gap one day". Little did I know I was speaking this into existence at the time, but she and I became close friends during college and developed a wonderful relationship. The lesson here was that definitions of others about you, does not have to define you.

In 2009 I was approached by a student who was trying to get into Pharmacy School. She said, "Dr. Sutton, I want to go to Pharmacy school, but no one will accept me."

I asked her why that was the case. And she said, "Because I am ugly and spit when I talk."

I told her she was not ugly and acknowledged that spitting while she talked would not disqualify her from attending pharmacy school. She was struggling with major self-esteem issues. I told her to look into her hand as if it were a mirror and to tell me what she saw.

She said, "I see an ugly, fat, kind of smart girl." I told her to flip her hand over and then tell me what she saw. She went on to say that she saw the same ugly girl. Finally, I told her to go wash her hands with a special soap in my office bathroom. When she returned I informed her that something about the soap in our bathroom changes people. She asked what was so special about the soap and my only answer was that it shows people who they really are and not what others say they are.

Once again, I asked her to look into her hand and tell me what she saw. This time she said she saw a nice looking girl wearing a pharmacy white coat who was smart, funny, and giving. What I showed her was no new person, just the same person stored behind all the layers of social labels placed on her. I often tell the students I speak to that if no one is willing to encourage you, it is okay to encourage yourself.

A famous gospel singer of the early 1950's, Mahalia Jackson, sang a song, "How did I make it over?" Many nights when I sit in my home, think of the many blessings I've received, look at the degrees on my wall, and drive to an office where I am the CEO, I ask myself, "How did I make it over"?

The answer is I made it over by the contribution of un-known heroes: a librarian at Jack Yates High School, a mother who made tough decisions, a father who guided me in his own way, family and friends who gave me the encouragement to climb mountains.

I was asked by a student, as I spoke to the premedical asso-ciation at the University of Washington, what I feel is my greatest attribute. I replied that my greatest attributes are not my legs, although they gave me the ability to walk to a place of safety and security at the Covenant House Homeless Shelter. My greatest attribute are not my eyes, even though they allow me to see the good in all people. My greatest attributes are my arms, because they have allowed me to reach for heights unimaginable. These same arms have provided me with the gift of reaching back and lifting others as I climb.

You are amazing, believe that. You are going to be successful, believe that. You will accomplish more than you ever imagined, believe that as well. Today is a new day and when someone ask you what's the reason for your smile. When they notice that different stride in your step and wonder what has changed about you, just let them know that it is HUSTLE time. Keep your eyes on handling your business, unlocking your purpose, stepping up to the plate, turning your mold into penicillin, leaping without regrets and encouraging yourself daily.

Good Luck and Congratulations.

Trouble Don't Last Always

My lights got cut off the other day

I was only a month past due on the bill

And they repossessed my car

Now you can imagine how I feel

The love of my life, my honey my squeeze has left me

And I'm walking around in a daze

But I'm holding on, because mama told me

Trouble don't last always

There is no food on the table

And my refrigerator and cabinets are bare

I went to see about food stamps

But you know nothing happening there

I really don't like this position

Feeling like I have to beg

But what else am I supposed to do

Knowing my kids have to be fed

I know what I'm going through

Ain't nothing but a phase

So I keep my mind on the words of mama

Trouble don't last always

Well my lights are on and I bought a new car

And there is a new love in my life

I've got money in my bank account

And my kids aren't hungry tonight

So I called my mama to tell her

And you know she was not amazed?

In fact she said, "The GOD I serve

Won't let trouble last always"

So when you're up against some trouble

And you're having some bad days

Remember that GOD has your back

And trouble won't last always.

written by Anthony Sutton 1991

CONCLUSION

As you read this book I hope it touched you in some way. Reflecting on my life and the life of others I realize that we all have our fair share of struggles. Your struggle may be overcoming test anxiety, deciding on whether to let a friendship go, or giving up some addiction like smoking, or alcohol. We have some iced mountains to climb. The good news is that you will climb them. It may not be the easiest ascent, but the view from the peak will allow you to really see how far you have come and offer a glimpse into where you are going.

Some have asked me how is the relationship between my dad and me. Wonderful. He stopped drinking many years ago and as always he continues to be a listening ear when I need one. Many people talk about hero's and refer to some mythical figure like Superman or Hercules. I can honestly say that my father and mother are my heroes. Without them I may not have learned how to become a good public speaker. Without them I may not have learned how to give unselfishly. Without them I may have never acquired the strength to stand up to the obstacles of life. If my father is the rock of the family then my mother is surely the mortar that has kept our family foundation together. Debra and Adell Cross opened my eyes in different ways. One by the rod and the other by the light, but through it all they never stopped loving us. Today mend a broken relationship. Today say I love you. If not a family member, say it to yourself.

APPENDIX

Dr. Sutton's message to the graduate school applicants.

As I travel across the United States speaking to students who are applying to medical, dental, and pharmacy school I am asked a barrage of questions. I thought it would be beneficial if I listed some of the most commonly asked questions from applicants and my response. Please keep in mind my response is solely my opinion. It does not represent the views and opinions of UT Houston Medical School or any of my other scholastic affiliations.

Question: What are some good questions to ask my interviewer?

Most students ask questions that look at the educational achievements of the school they are applying to. This is okay, but at this point the school is trying to feel you out as an applicant and you are trying to feel the school out as a the potential place of your next stage of learning. As bad as this may sound and some will probably not like me saying this, but you need the school more than the school needs you. Yes the school wants the best applicant and yes you may be the best applicant, but with over 2,000 students applying at times, it would make more since if you connected with your interviewer in a real way. What I mean is that you could ask the interviewer how has their career changed since they began. Most interviewers love reliving that time in their life. They began to have those nostalgic moments and before you know it they have spent the better portion of the interview talking about something they enjoy, their career. When your interviewer begins to write their evaluation, you are more likely to receive a favorable evaluation if the interviewer had pleasant memories of your encounter. I am sure most interviewers will not admit they enjoy having a conversation that opens them up to the applicant, but some would be honest and admit this truth.

Question: Should I contact my interviewer after my interview?

There are mixed opinions on this, but one thing is for sure, you should definitely send them a thank you card. Many interviewers volunteer their time to interview students, so a thank you card would be a wonderful gesture. A thank you card could also be the difference in you getting a 5 out of 5 versus a 4 out of 5 on your evaluation. Is it mandatory to give a thank you card, no, but there is no harm in giving one. Make sure you hand write the card and have it delivered to the interviewer within three days.

Question: What is more important, getting experience in the field I am applying to, or increasing my non-health related volunteer hours?

Both of these experiences are important. I would suggest you have more than 50 hours in each area. Keep in mind that healthcare shadowing shows your commitment to healthcare, but volunteering in other areas outside of healthcare shows your commitment to people.

Question: How important is the personal essay in my application?

The essay is one of the few ways the admissions can find out who you are. This offers a brief time machine of your life. Things that should always be in the essay are; sentences that show you can get along with others. You can indicate this by highlighting your participation in various organization or activities. In your essay you should include language that indicates your commitment to the field. This can be done by showing experience you have had in the field. Most importantly, you should make sure the first and last paragraph are powerful. Anything you really want the admissions committee to know, make sure you put it in one of these paragraphs. The first sentence of your essay needs to really hook the reader into wanting to know more about you. A few examples of opening sentences are:

1. Growing up in a violent Washington D.C. neighbor-hood, I found my calling to medicine in an odd way.

2. At the age of 9 I began my career as a dentist.

These examples have the interviewer wanting to know more about you.

Question: If I have a low grade point average, should I give up on my dreams of being accepted?

No, but grades do matter. Many admissions committee members believe that your gpa shows how disciplined you are as a student. Yes, you may have gotten off to a slow start, but how did you perform over the last 60 hours. I would recommend that if your gpa is not where you want it, make the commitment today to turn it around. I had a semester in college where my gpa was a .55 and although it took me some time, I was able to show I could do the work and eventually got accepted into medical school. Never give up and don't listen to people who say you cannot do it. The only voice that matters is yours.

Question: If I am a freshman or senior in high school, but I know I want to become a dentist, physician, or pharmacist, what is the best way to prepare?

First, there is a book called *Study Without Stress* by Kathleen Straker. This is a good starting point. Below is a step-wise approach that has helped students in the past.

- ❖ **Year 1 semester 1** – Meet with your college advisors. Recommended classes (Biology 1 and Chemistry 1 in addition to any classes required for your degree plan)

- ❖ Choose a degree that you enjoy even if that means it's not biology or chemistry. It's more important that you have a great gpa than for you to have a1000 hours of genetics or microbiology. In the past I have interviewed students with degrees in music, art history, economics etc.

❖ Get a hold of the study material for the exam you are preparing for. If you are taking the MCAT/DAT/PCAT or OAT in a few years get the study material from respected companies. Use this material in conjunction with your corresponding classes. That means if you are taking general chemistry, then when you are covering acids and bases in class, write notes in your Prep book regarding what you learned in class. This same book will become your study guide later.

❖ Begin volunteer activities outside of the healthcare field. Good examples would be food banks, homeless shelters, monitoring booths at local walks for a cause and the list goes on. If you are interested in some volunteer ideas call (713) 244-4524.

❖ Begin putting things into your shoebox

❖ Assume some leadership within your University. Leadership does not mean you have to be the president of the organization or secretary. It means that you have been instrumental in organizing some activity or event. It means that you have shown the ability to create and execute a task while interacting with others.

❖ Position yourself to gain scholastic achievement which can range from making the dean's list to receiving an academic scholarship. There are other types of academic achievements such as; best student in Organic Chemistry, recognition for most improved in Microbiology. Any certificate, or invitation to an organization based on academic performance should go into your shoebox.

❖ Gain healthcare experiences which show some hands on experience that was meaningful to you. It is important that you convey to admissions department that you truly understand what you are getting yourself into. Many students have asked me over the years, "How many hours of shadowing do I need"? There is no magic number, but in my opinion, 40 hours would be a minimum. Be sure to make the most out of every shadowing experience. Those you shadow may one day be the one you ask to write a recommendation letter on your behalf.

❖ Get to know your college instructors personally. Make positive impressions because these too will be individuals who will write a letter on your behalf.

❖ Developing a good study method early in your college career is important and could prove to be monumental in your preparation for exams. Remember that Intelligent Effort = Intelligent Results.

❖ Be sure to start researching the schools you would like to attend by looking up their websites and contacting their admissions department. For a list of schools go to:

- ❖ Medical school admissions visit: https://www.aamc.org/students/applying/requirements/admissions_offices/

- ❖ Dental school admissions visit: http://www.ada.org/267.aspx

- ❖ Pharmacy school admissions visit: http://www.aacp.org/about/membership/institutionalmembership/Pages/usinstitutionalmember.asp

- ❖ Optometry school admissions visit: http://www.tcnj.edu/~biology/7med/Listofoptometryschools_000.htm

- ❖ Keep in mind that what we recommend this as an outline and should not supersede the advice of your university advisors. They are ultimately the ones who will work with you daily.

- ❖ **Year 1 semester 2 –** Recommended classes (Chemistry 2 and Math course in addition to any courses for your degree plan).

- ❖ Continue to add items to your shoebox.

- ❖ Begin tutoring a student who is taking one of the science classes you have already taken. This will help you to retain the information you have already learned. It can also be listed as a leadership activity on your application.

- ❖ Find a pre-health organization to join

- ❖ **End of year 1 summer activities** - Seek out summer research opportunities that interest you. Prior to conducting research, ask the primary investigator if there would be an opportunity for you to be published. Don't do any research that you are not interested in because when it comes time to explain to an admissions officer, your lack of enthusiasm will usually shine through. After completing the research, be sure to add the activity to the shoebox.

❖ **Year 2 semester 1** – Recommended classes (Organic 1 and Physics 1 if possible in addition to any courses for you degree plan).

❖ Continue to stay involved and participate in an event that allows you to interact in a multicultural environment. Examples may include working at the International Festival or assisting other cultural diverse organizations with some of their activities.

❖ Complete winter exam prep. This can be done on your own or as a part of a course. You should treat this time as if your test were in January. This will allow you to identify any week areas you may have missed during your first year and half. It will also serve to prepare you for the spring and summer months.

❖ **Year 2 semester 2** – Recommended classes (Organic 2 and Physics 2 if possible in addition to any courses for your degree plan).

❖ Continue all the aforementioned activities such as volunteering, community service etc.

❖ Seek shadowing opportunities in your chosen field.

❖ Create something new. This could be a new organization that addresses how to prevent smoking in public places. It could be an arts program for underprivileged youth or setting up an on-campus adoption program for abandoned animals. These are just suggestions, but this is the time to use your creativity. Not only does this show leadership, but it show you have a heart.

About the Author

Dr. Sutton is a highly requested motivational speaker and workshop facilitator. He received his medical degree from UT Houston Medical School. He is a medical consultant and CEO of MDI Prep Corporation. As CEO of MDI, he has helped the company grow from one student in 2009 to over two hundred students in 2012.

Prior to entering the school of medicine Dr. Sutton served as a Beaumont Police Officer and Harris County Officer for 10 years. He has been the President of the Black Police Officers Association and Student National Medical Association and Director of the Youth Leadership Forum. Dr. Sutton is a frequent speaker at the University of Houston, Texas Southern University, University of Washington (Seattle), UT Austin, and Prairie View A&M University to name a few.

He has served on the board for the Houston Homeless Coalition and Safety Coalition for the UT Health Science Center. He was the invited speaker for Covenant House International in New York City, honoring for former first lady's Barbara and Laura Bush.

Dr. Sutton is a member of the American Medical Association and a medical school admissions interviewer. He is an active member of Omega Psi Phi Fraternity, has three wonderful children and is an avid golfer.